CHRONOLOGICAL LIST OF ENGAGEMENTS

AMS PRESS

NEW YORK

GEORGE W. WEBB
Company G, 3rd U. S. Infantry,
1873 - 1874

CHRONOLOGICAL

LIST OF ENGAGEMENTS

BETWEEN THE REGULAR ARMY OF THE

UNITED STATES AND VARIOUS TRIBES OF

HOSTILE INDIANS WHICH OCCURRED

DURING THE YEARS

1790 to 1898, INCLUSIVE.

By
GEORGE W. WEBB

a / 8 2 5 8

Library of Congress Cataloging in Publication Data

Webb, George Washington, 1856-1938, comp.
    Chronological list of engagements between the Regular
Army of the United States and various tribes of hostile
Indians which occurred during the years 1790 to 1898,
inclusive.

    Reprint of the 1939 ed. published by Wing Print.
and Pub. Co,. St. Joseph, Mo.
    1. Indians of North America—Wars. 2. United
States—History, Military—To 1900. I. Title:
Chronological list of engagements between the Regular
Army of the United States. . . .
E81.W42   1976   973   74-15125
ISBN 0-404-11984-0

E
81
·W42
1976

From the edition of 1939, St. Joseph, Mo.
First AMS edition published in 1976
Manufactured in the United States of America

AMS PRESS INC.
NEW YORK, N. Y.

DEDICATION

In memory of George W. Webb, editor, friend and staunch aid to Indian War Veterans, we have completed this book compiled by him in his last years, and to him we now dedicate this volume.

Tell me not in mournful numbers,
   Life is but an empty dream!
For the soul is dead that slumbers
   And things are not what they seem.

Life is real! Life is earnest!
   And the grave is not its goal;
Dust thou art, to dust returnest,
   Was not spoken of the soul.

Not enjoyment and not sorrow,
   Is our destined end or way;
But to act that each tomorrow
   Finds us farther than today.

* * *

In the world's broad field of battle,
   In the bivouac of Life,
Be not like dumb, driven cattle!
   Be a hero in the strife!

* * *

Lives of great men all remind us
   We can make our lives sublime
And, departing, leave behind us
   Foot prints on the sands of time;

Footprints, that perhaps another,
   Sailing o'er life's solemn main,
A forlorn and shipwrecked brother
   Seeing shall take heart again.

Let us then be up and doing
   With a heart for any fate;
Still achieveing, still pursuing,
   Learn to labor and to wait.

          — Longfellow's "Psalm of Life"

BIOGRAPHY
OF
COMRADE GEORGE W. WEBB

Comrade George W. Webb was the son of Julia Rowles and John Webb. He was born at Albia, Iowa, January 20, 1856.

Comrade Webb followed in the foot-steps of his father, who was a Captain of the Iowa Volunteers in the Civil War, when he ran away at the age of 17 and enlisted in Company G, 3rd U. S. Infantry, under the name of George W. West. He was sworn in at Ft. Leavenworth, Kansas, by Gen. Nelson A. Miles, on April 1, 1873, and was discharged September 25, 1874, at Jackson Barracks, Louisiana.

From New Orleans he worked his way north and arrived in St. Joseph, Missouri, in January, 1875. After a brief stay with his sister here he went farther north to Janesville, Wisconsin, where he remained until October, 1877. The years 1878 to 1880 were spent at Dubuque, and Cedar Rapids, Iowa, and Minneapolis, Minnesota.

From Minneapolis he went down in the orange country of Florida, where he helped establish several towns. He remained there until May, 1888, at which time one of the worst freezes that country had ever known ruined his orange groves and forced him out of business.

He returned to St. Joseph and assisted in installing a Street Railway System.

In December of 1889 he went to Denver, Colorado, as superintendent of the first Electric Street Railway of that city. Because of ill health, he was forced to give up his work there in May, 1890, and after a brief visit to his home town of Albia, Iowa, he returned to St. Joseph in August of that year.

After his return to St. Joseph he became affiliated with the Knights and Ladies of Security as their organizer and district manager, a position he held for a number of years. He was also associated with Capt. John Duncan in the management of the Smith Estate for 25 years, and it was this work that he gave up when failing health forced him to remain at home.

It was at this time that he became interested in the pension problems of the Indian War Veterans and Widows. Due to his business ability he was able to organize the Indian War Veterans into a strong national body, and to publish in their behalf the paper, "Winners of the West." This was in 1923. Mr. Webb continued to edit and publish this paper up to the time of his death October 28, 1938. Since he first took up the work the pensions of the Indian War Veterans were raised from a set rate of $20 per month, regardless of age, disabilities, etc., to a step rate pension from a rate of $25 per month at age 62 to $55 per month at age 75 and a total disability pension of $72 per month.

The widows' pensions were raised from $12 per month to $30 per month.

In all of this work his hand was at the rudder ever guiding a straight course. This in spite of poor health.

In addition to his business activities he was an active church worker and a deeply religious man. He was a charter member of the First Reformed Church, founded in 1891, and was one of its first elders. He not only worked in the church but carried the teachings of Christianity into his business and everyday life. He always tried to "Do unto others as ye would have them do unto you."

His vast experience in life well qualified him to give advice and counsel to all who came to him, and there were many who sought him out.

A fellow co-worker of Mr. Webb's once said of him: "George Webb was a great friend to the young man (and woman) stepping out of school into a world of which he knew little.

"He advised and aided many such a young person until they became well versed in affairs of state and nation and developed into good citizens and successful business men.

"I fondly recall past memories and happy associations, and knowing George Webb, can picture the Great Master saying, "Enter into thy heavenly home; thy work on earth is well done, thou good and faithful servant."

> "The years may wipe out many things
> But this they wipe out never,
> The memory of those happy days
> When we were associated together."

CHRONOLOGICAL LIST OF ENGAGEMENTS BETWEEN THE REGULAR ARMY OF THE UNITED STATES AND VARIOUS TRIBES OF HOSTILE INDIANS WHICH OCCURRED DURING THE YEARS 1790 TO 1898, INCLUSIVE

NOTE——Regular regiments mentioned prior to 1815 are not identical with regiments of the same numbers as now existing.

1790

October 19 .... On Eel River, Indiana, 11 miles from present Fort Wayne, Ind. Lt. Col. Commandant Josiah Harmar with 30 men, 1st Infantry and Kentucky volunteers against 100 Indians under Little Turtle of the Miamis. 22 regulars killed.

October 22 .... Near confluence of the St. Joseph and St. Mary's Rivers, Indiana (now Fort Wayne, Ind.) Lt. Col. Com. Josiah Harmar; 60 men, 1st Infantry, Maj. J. P. Wyllys; militia, Maj. J. C. Hall; Maj. M'Mullin's battalion; Maj. Fontaine's cavalry. Major Wyllys killed. In the entire expedition, including the above two battles, casualties were 183 killed, 31 wounded.

1791

November 4 .... Near sources of the Miami of the Lakes, and near site of Fort Recovery, Ohio (St. Clair's defeat)—Maj. Gen. Arthur St. Clair; Regiment of Artillerists; 1st Infantry (?); 2nd Infantry; 350 Kentucky militiamen, Lt. Col. Oldham, Peter Faulkner's Rifle Company; cavalry, against a force of 2,000 Miamis, Delawares, Shawanoes, Wyandots, Ottawas, Chippewas, Potawatomis, led by Red Jacket of the Shawanoes, Buck-ong-a-helos of the Delawares, and Simon Girty. Casualties; 632 killed and 264 wounded of a total force of 1,400.

1793

October 17 .... Seven miles beyond Fort St. Clair, Ohio, while escorting a train of provision wagons. 1st and 2nd Sublegions, Legion of the United States. Lieut. John Lowry and 14 men killed.

1794

June 30 .... Fort Recovery, Wabash River, Ohio—Squadron, Light Dragoons; 1st, 2nd, 3rd, 4th Sublegions.

August 20 .... Fallen Timbers, Rapids of the Miami of Lake Erie, Ohio—Corps of Artillerists and Engineers; Squadron Light Dragoons; 1st, 2nd, 3rd, 4th Sublegions; 1,600 mounted volunteers from Kentucky, under Maj. Gen. Anthony Wayne against Indians under Little Turtle.

1811

November 7 .... Tippecanoe, near Prophet's Town, Ind. (now Battle Ground, near LaFayette, Ind.) 4th Infantry, one company 7th Infantry, one company Riflemen, 60 Kentucky volunteers, 600 Indiana militia, under Brig. Gen. William Henry Harrison against Shawanoes Wyandots, Kickapoos, Ottawas, Chippewas, Potawatomies, Winnebagoes, Sacs, Miamis, under Elkswatawa (the Prophet).

War of 1812

NOTE——Indians were employed by the British in many of the campaigns of the War of 1812, particularly in the west. Those in which British troops were also engaged are marked with a *. No attempt is made to list all conflicts in which Indians may have taken part.

1812

July 17 .... *Fort Michilimackinac, Mich., surrender—Detachment of 1st Artillery.

August 9 .... *Maguagua, Oak Woods, or Brownstown, Mich.—Detachment, Regiment of Artillerists; Detachments 1st and 4th Infantry.

August 15—16 .... *Siege and surrender of Detroit, Mich. Detachment of Artillery. Detachment of 1st and 4th U. S. Infty.

August 15 .... Fort Dearborn, Ill. (Chicago)—One company, 1st Infantry, 54 men under Capt. Nathan Heald, against Potawatomis under Black Bird. 26 soldiers, 112 citizens, killed.

September 4—5 .... Fort Harrison, Ind. (Vincennes)—One company, 7th Infantry, 50 men. Capt. Zachary Taylor in command.

September 5—12 .... Fort Wayne, Ind., siege of—One company, 1st Infantry. 70 men under Capt. James Rhea.

September 5—8 .... Fort Madison, Bellevue, Ill.—Detachment, 1st Infantry. Lieutenants Hamilton and Vasquez in command.

December 17—18 .... Mississinewa River, Ind. (near Marion, Ind.)— One Company, 2nd Light Dragoons, Capt. Wilson Elliott, Maj. James V. Ball; One company, 19th Infantry, Lt. Col. John B. Campbell; Butler's Pittsburg Blues; Alexander's Pennsylvania Riflemen, against Miami and Delaware Indians. 8 Indians killed, 40 captured.

1813

January 18 .... *Frenchtown, on the River Raisin, Mich.—One company, 17th Infantry.

January 22 .... *Frenchtown, Mich.—Three companies, 17th Infantry; One Company, 19th Infantry.

April 28—May 9 .... *Siege of Fort Meigs, on the Maumee River, Ohio—1st Light Dragoons, Detachment 1st Artillery, 17th and 19th Infantry.

May 5 ....*Fort Meigs, Ohio, capture of Clay's detachment—Detachment 1st Artillery.

August 2 .... Fort Stephenson, Ohio (Lower Sandusky). Detachment 17th and 24th Infantry.

October 4 .... *Chatham, Upper Canada. 120 men, 27th Infantry.

October 5 .... *Thames River, Upper Canada—120 men, 27th Infantry, volunteers of Army of the West, Maj. Gen. W. H. Harrison against Proctor's British and Tecumseh's Indians. Tecumseh killed.

December 23 .... Econachaca, The Holy Ground, Ala.,—Detachment 3rd Infantry under Col. Gilbert C. Russell; Volunteers; Militia; Choctaw scouts, under Maj. Gen. Andrew Jackson, against Creeks.

1814

March 27 .... Sehopiska (Horse Shoe Bend), Ala.—39th Infantry, Mississippi, Tennessee, Georgia and Alabama volunteers under Maj. Gen. Andrew Jackson against Creeks led by William Weatherford (Red Eagle).

NOTE——Other fights of Creek War, involving volunteers and militia were; 1813, July 27, Burnt Corn Creek; August 3, Fort Mims massacre; November 3, Tallesehatche; November 9, Talledega; November 18, Hillabee; November 24, Auttose; 1814, January 21, Emucfau; January 24, Enocochopio Creek; January 26, Calabee River.

July 19 .... Rapids of the Mississippi, near Rock River, Ill. Detachment of 1st Infantry; Detachment of Rangers.

July 20 .... Surrender at Prairie du Chien, Wis. One company, 7th Infantry; Indian allies. Lt. Col. M'Kay in command.

August 4 .... Fort Michilimackinac, Mich. Corps of Artillery; 24th Infantry. Detachments of 17th and 19th Infantry.

September 5 .... Near mouth of Rock River, Ill. Detachment of 7th Infantry.

NOTE——Subsequent to the War of 1812 the Regular Army was recognized in such a manner that few modern organizations can be traced directly to organizations existing prior to that date.

In 1814 the two regiments of Light Dragoons were consolidated, and in 1815 the Regiment of Light Dragoons was consolidated with the Corps of Artillery, leaving the army without mounted troops.

In 1814 the Artillerists, the 2nd Artillery and the 3rd Artillery, were reorganized as a Corps of Artillery. In 1815 the 41st, 42nd and 43rd Infantry and the Dragoons were consolidated with the Corps of Artillery, while the Regiment of Light Artillery absorbed Infantry Regiments with the following numbers: 15, 26, 30, 31, 33, 34, 45. In 1821 four regiments of Artillery were organized from the Corps of Artillery and the Regiment of Light Artillery. These regiments endured until 1901 when they were again consolidated as an Artillery Corps, which became the Coast Artillery Corps when regiments of Field Artillery were organized in 1907. In 1924 the old regiments of 1821-1901 were re-constituted, as far as possible, as regiments of Coast Artillery, many of the old batteries retaining their original letters.

In 1815 eight regiments of Infantry and one of riflemen were organized from regiments then existing as follows:

1st Infantry from the 2nd, 3rd, 7th and 44th.

2nd Infantry from the 6th, 16th, 22nd, 23rd and 32nd.

3rd Infantry from the 1st, 17th, 19th, 24th, 28th and 39th.
4th Infantry from the 12th, 14th and 20th.
5th Infantry from the 4th, 9th, 13th, 21st, 40th and 46th.
6th Infantry from the 11th, 25th, 27th, 29th, and 37th.
7th Infantry from the 8th, 10th, 36th and 38th.
8th Infantry from the 5th, 18th, and 35th (dropped 1832, reorganized 1838).
1st Riflemen from the 1st, 2nd, 3rd, and 4th Riflemen. Discharged, 1821.

Indian Campaigns

1815

May 24 .... Near site of Fort Howard, Wis. One company of Rangers.

1817

November 23 .... Fowltown, Ga. 300 officers and enlisted men, 1st, 4th and 7th Infantry.

November 30 .... Apalachicola River, Fla. 40 officers and enlisted men, 4th and 7th Infantry. Lieut. Richard W. Scott, 7th Infantry, and seven women massacred by Seminoles.

December 15—16 .... Apalachicola River, Fla. 30 miles below Fort Scott, Ga. 120 officers and enlisted men, 4th and 7th Infantry.

1818

April .... Escambia River, Ala. Detachment of 8th Infantry.

April 25 .... Near Bayou Texas, Pensacola Bay, Fla. Detachment of 8th Infantry.

May 26—27 .... Fort Barrancas, Fla. One company, Corps of Artillery; Detachment of 4th Infantry.

1823

August 9—11 .... Arickaree Towns, Missouri River. 700 miles above Council Bluffs. Cos. A, B, D, E, F, G, 6th Infantry.

1832

August 1 .... Near mouth of Bad Axe River, Ill. 16 men, 4th Infantry.

August 2 .... Bad Axe River, Ill. (Near its junction with the Mississippi River), Cos. A, B, G, K. 1st Infantry; Co. F, 5th Infantry; Cos. A, B, C, D, E, G, I, K, 6th Infantry. Against Black Hawk's band of Sacs and Foxes.

1835

December 28 .... Near Withlacoochie River, Fla. Bats. B, C, H, 2nd Artillery; Bat. B, 3rd Artillery; Co. B, 4th Infantry. Bvt. Maj. Francis L. Dade, 4th Inf. in command. Against Seminoles under Oseola and Micanopy. 107 killed, 3 escaped.

December 31 .... Ford of Withlacoochie River, Fla. Bat. C, 1st Artillery; Bats. D, F, 2nd Artillery; Bats. C, H, 3rd Artillery; Co. D, 4th Infantry; 500 volunteers.

1836

January 12 .... Fort King, Fla. Bat. I, 1st Artillery.

February 27—March 5 .... Camp Izard. Ford of Withlacoochie River, Fla. Bats. A, B, G, H, 2nd Artillery; Cos. A, B, E, G, H, I, K, 4th Infantry.

March 30 .... Okahumpka Swamp, Fla. Bats. A, E, G, H, 1st Artillery.

March 31 .... Oloklikaha, on Withlacoochie River, Fla. Detachment of 2nd Dragoons; Bats. C, H, I, 3rd Artillery; Cos. A, B, D, E, G, H, I, K, 4th Infantry.

April 12 .... Ft. Barnwell, Volusia, Fla. Detachment of 1st Artillery; Detachment of 4th Infantry.

April 26—27 .... Thlonotosassa Creek, Fla. Detachment of Bat. G, 2nd Artillery; Cos. A, B, D, E, G, H, I, K, 4th Infantry.

May 8 .... Matanzas, near Hernandez Plantation, Fla. Bat. D, 1st Artillery.

June 9 .... Micanopy, Fla. Tr. D, 2nd Dragoons; Detachments of Bats. D, E, 2nd Artillery; Detachments of Bats. C, H, I, 3rd Artillery.

July 19 .... Welika Pond, Fla. Detachment of Tr. D, 2nd Dragoons; Bats. C, F, 1st Artillery; Bats. D, F, 2nd Artillery; Bats. C, H, I, 3rd Artillery.

July 27 .... Ridgley's Mills, Fla. Detachments of Bats. A, D, 1st Artillery.

August 21 .... Ft. Drane, Fla. Detachment of Tr. D, 2nd Dragoons; Bats. C, D, E, F, G, 1st Artillery; Bats. A, C, H, I, 3rd Artillery; Bat. C, 4th Artillery.

September 18 .... San Velasco Hammock, near Ft. Gilliland, Fla. Detachment of Bat. B, 1st Artillery.

September 30 .... Near Tampa Bay, Fla. Detachment of 2nd Artillery.

November 21 .... Wahoo Swamp, east bank of the Withlacoochie River, Fla. Bats. A, B, E, G, H, 1st Artillery; Bats. E, F, 2nd Artillery; Bats. A, C, H, and I, 3rd Artillery; Bat. H, 4th Artillery.

1837

January 15 .... Camp Clinch, Fla. Co. K, 4th U. S. Infty. Captain G. W. Allen in command. Indians captured, 21.

January 27 .... Hatcheeluskee Creek, near Great Cypress Swamp, Fla. Detachment of Co. E, 4th U. S. Artillery.

February 8 .... Camp Monroe, Fla. Cos. E, G, & H, 2nd Dragoons; Co. C, 2nd Artillery; and Co. B, 3rd Artillery. Lieut. Col. A. C. W. Fanning in Command. Capt. Charles Mellon killed. Soldiers wounded, 11.

February 9 .... Clear River, Fla. Co. K, 4th U. S. Infty. Capt. Geo. W. Allen in command. Officers killed, 1.

September 10 .... Mosquito Inlet (near St. Augustine, Fla.) Detachments of Cos. E, F, & H, 2nd Dragoons; Co. D, 3rd Artillery and Mounted Florida volunteers. Lieuts. John W. S. McNeil and Chas. A. May in command. Lieut. McNeil killed. Indians captured, 35.

December 25 .... Lake Okeechobee, Fla. Co. G, 4th U. S. Artillery; Cos. A, B, C, D, E, F, G, H, & K, 1st Infty.; Cos. A, B, C, D, E, G, & I, 4th Infty; Cos. A, B, F, G, H, I, & K, 6th U. S. Infty. Col. Zachary Taylor, 1st U. S. Infty; Lieut. Col. Wm. Davenport, 1st U. S. Infty. Lieut. Col. Wm. Foster, 4th U. S. Infty., in command. Lieut. Col. A. R. Thompson, Capt. Joseph Van Swearingen, 1st Lieut. F. J. Brooke, and Lieut. John P. Center, 6th Infty., killed in this engagement. Soldiers killed, 26. Soldiers wounded, 112.

1838

January 15 .... Near Mouth of Jupiter Inlet, Fla. Co. I, 1st U. S. Artillery. Capt. F. Whiting in command. Lieut. W. H. Fowler, 1st Artillery, wounded. Soldiers killed, 2. Soldiers wounded, 11.

January 24 .... Indian Crossing of the Lochahatchie, Fla. Cos. A, B, D, E, G, I, & K, 2nd Dragoons; Cos. A, B, C, D, E, F, H, & I, 3rd Artillery; Cos. B, D, & H, 4th Artillery. Gen. Abram Eustis, Col. D. E. Twiggs, Col. William Gates in command. Soldiers killed, 2. Soldiers wounded, 5. Indians captured, 40. Engagement was with the Seminole Indians.

March 23 .... The Everglades, Fla. Cos. A, B, D, F, G, & H, 1st Artillery; Co. D, 3rd Artillery; Cos. D, & H, 4th Artillery.

April 29 .... Tuscawilla Pond (near Micanopy, Fla.) Co. I, 4th Artillery; Detachment of Recruits. Brevet Major J. Erwine in command. Soldiers killed, 2 Soldiers wounded, 2.

May 20 .... Near Ft. Clinch, Fla. Co. G, 2nd Artillery.

June 17 .... Kenahapa Prairie, Fla. Detachments of Co. C and F, 2nd Dragoons. Capt. L. J. Beall in command. Soldiers wounded, 6. Detachment of 30 soldiers attacked by Seminole Indians.

August 16 .... Near Fort Norton, Georgia. Detachment of Co. F, 2nd Dragoons. Soldiers killed, 1. Soldiers wounded, 2.

November 1 .... North Carolina Mountains, N. C. Detachment of Co. I, 4th U. S. Infty. Lieut. Col. William Foster in command. Soldiers killed, 2.

December 27 .... Econfina River, Fla. Detachment of Co. E, 6th U. S. Infty. Soldiers wounded, 1. The Indians attacked the Camp Guard.

1839

February 11 .... New River Inlet, Fla. Co. K, 3rd Artillery.

February 20 .... Near Ft. Lauderdale, Fla. Detachment of Co. K, 3rd Artillery. Capt. William B. Davidson in command. Soldiers killed, 2 Killed while cutting wood.

February 28 .... Ft. Miami, Fla. Detachment of Co. I, 2nd U. S. Infty. Capt. S. L. Russell in command. Capt. Russell was killed. Soldiers wounded, 1.

March 20 .... Etonia Scrub, Fla. Detachment of Co. H, 2nd U. S. Infty. Capt. John Mackay, captain of engineers, in command. Soldiers killed, 1.

May 2 .... Near Ft. Frank Brooke, Fla. Co. F, 6th U. S. Infty. Lieut. Wm. Hulbert killed by Indians at 14 mile Creek.

May 20 .... Between Fts. No. 3 and No. 4, Fla. Detachment of Co. K, 7th U. S. Infty. Capt J. B. Davis in command. One soldier killed while riding the Express.

July 21 .... Between Fts. Brooke and Andrews, Fla. Detachment of Co. F, 6th U. S. Infty. 1st Lieut. J. B. Todd in command. One soldier killed while riding the Express.

July 23 .... Caloosahatchee River, Fla., trading house, 7 miles above Charlotte Harbor. Detachments of Cos. A, C, D, E, and F, 2nd Dragoons. Col. D. E. Twiggs, in command. Lieut. Col. W. S. Harney and 14 men escaped. Ten were reported missing. Sergt. Bigelow and Corporal Haywood, 5 soldiers and 1 citizen were killed.

August 29 .... Near Fort Andrews, Fla. Detachment of Co. I, 6th U. S. Infty. Capt. Geo. Andrews in command. Soldiers killed, 2. Soldiers were surprised by the Indians.

September 10 .... Near Fort Fanning, Fla. Detachment Co. D, 1st U. S. Infty. Capt. T. Parker in command. Soldiers killed, 1. Soldiers wounded, 1.

September 27 .... Ft. Lauderdale, Fla. Detachment of Bat. K, 3rd U. S. Artillery. Capt. W. B. Davidson in command. Two soldiers killed while cutting wood.

November 25 .... Between St. Augustine and Picolata, Fla. Co. K, 3rd Artillery.

1840

January 21 .... Near Suwannee, Fla. Co. B, 1st U. S. Infty.

January 24 .... Ft. New Smyrna, Fla. Co. B, 3rd U. S. Artillery. Capt. J. R. Vinton in command. Soldiers wounded, 4.

January 24 .... Near Ft. Preston, Fla. Detachment of Co. E, 2nd Dragoons. Capt. E. D. Bullock in command. Soldiers wounded, 1. Indians attacked a wagon guard.

February 1 .... Near Ft. No. 5, Fla. Detachment of Co. C, 7th U. S. Infty. Capt. H. H. Holmes in command. Soldiers killed, 1. Soldiers wounded, 2.

February 10 .... Near Ft. No. 3, Fla. Co. H, 7th U. S. Infty.

March 15 .... Near Ft. Drane, Fla. Detachment of Co. B, 7th U. S. Infty. Lieut. W. K. Hanson in command. Soldiers wounded, 1.

March 24 .... Near Fort King, Fla. Detachment of Co. A, 7th U. S. Infty. Capt. G. J. Rains in command. Soldiers killed, 2.

April 10 .... Near Ft. Wool, Fla. Co. I, 2nd Dragoons. Capt. B. L. Beall in command. Soldiers wounded, 1.

April 12 .... Between Fts. Griffin and Fanning, Fla. Detachments of Cos. C and I, 6th U. S. Infty. Soldiers wounded, 1. Escort to wagon train.

April 14 .... Near Ft. King, Fla. Detachment of Co. A, 7th U. S. Infty. Capt. G. J. Rains in command. Soldiers killed, 2.

April 24 .... Near Ft. Lauderdale, Fla. Detachment of Co. K, 3rd Artillery. Capt. W. D. Davidson in command. Soldiers wounded, 4.

April 25 .... Near Fort Barker, Fla. Detachment of Co. I, 1st Infty. Soldiers killed, 1; he died of wounds.

April 28 .... Near Ft. King, Fla. Co. A, 7th U. S. Infty. Lieut. J. R. Scott in command. Soldiers killed, 1. Soldiers wounded, 3.

May 19 ....Near Micanopy, Fla. Detachment of Co. K, 2nd U. S. Infty. Lieut. J. W. Martin in command. Lieut. Martin wounded. Soldiers killed, 2. Indians captured, 1.

May 19 .... Levy's Prairie, 8 miles from Micanopy, Fla. Detachment of Cos. F, H, & I, 7th U. S. Infty. Lieut. J. S. Sanderson in command. Lieut. Sanderson killed. Soldiers killed, 5. Soldiers wounded, 1.

July 12 .... Cow Creek Hammock, near Ft. Brady, Fla. Co. B, 2nd U. S. Infty. Capt. J. R. Smith in command. Soldiers killed, 2.

July 13 .... Near Econfina River, Fla. Detachment of Co. B, and of Co. D, 6th U. S. Infty. Soldiers killed, 2. Soldiers wounded, 1. Indians attacked a wagon escort.

July 16 .... Near Fort Russell, Fla. Detachment of Co. I, 2nd Dragoons. Capt. B. L. Beall in command. Soldiers wounded, 2.

July 24 .... Wekiva River, Fla. Detachment of Cos. A & F, 2nd Dragoons. Sergeant C. O. Willis in command. Soldiers killed, 1. The Indians attacked a horse guard of 16 soldiers.

July 26 .... New River Inlet, Fla. Detachment of Co. K, 3rd Artillery.

August 13 .... Near Fort Wheelock, Fla. Detachments of Cos. A & C, 7th U. S. Infty. Soldiers killed, 2. Soldiers wounded, 1.

August 30 .... Near Fort Micanopy, Fla. Detachment of Cos. E & I, 7th U. S. Infty. Soldiers killed, 3.

September 6 .... Near Ft. Wacahoota, Fla. Detachments of Cos. B & H, 7th U. S. Infty. Soldiers killed, 1. Soldiers wounded 3.

November 1 .... Near Picolata, Fla. Co. G, 3rd Artillery. Capt. Hezekiah Garner in command. Soldiers killed, 2.

December 3-24 .... The Everglades, Fla. Detachments of Cos. A, B, D, F, H, & K, 2nd Dragoons; Cos. D, H, I, & K, 3rd Artillery; and Negro Guides. Lieut. Col. Wm. S. Harney, Co. K, 2nd Dragoons, and Major T. T. Fauntleroy, 2nd Dragoons, in command. Soldiers killed, 1. Soldiers wounded, 1. 25 men each from each Co. H, 11 from Co. I and 33 from Co. H, 3rd Artillery took part in the engagement.

December 28 .... Martin's Point Hammock near Micanopy, Fla. Detachments of Cos. C, E, and I, 7th U. S. Infty. Lieut. W. Sherwood in command. Lieut. Sherwood killed. Soldiers killed, 4.

1841

January 7 .... Near Ft. Lauderdale, Fla. Co. I, 3rd U. S. Artillery. Capt. H. Burke in command. Soldiers killed, 1.

March 2 ....Orange Creek Bridge, near Fort Brooke, Fla. Co. K, 2nd U. S. Infty. Lieut. Wm. Alburtis in command. Soldiers killed, 3. Soldiers wounded, 6. There were 2 engagements, 22 men in one and 17 in the other, against 70 to 100 Indians. One man missing, supposed to be killed.

March 4 .... Ocklawaha River, Fla. Co. D, 2nd U. S. Infty. Capt. E. K. Barnum in command. Soldiers wounded, 2.

July 16 .... Near Ocklawaha River, Fla. Detachment of Co. C, 7th Infty; Co. D, 8th U. S. Infty. Soldiers killed, 1.

July 17 .... Camp Ogden, Pease Creek, Fla. Co. H, 8th U. S. Infty. Lieut. G. H. Hansen in command. Soldiers killed, 1.

September 29 .... 12 miles North of Ft. Russell, Fla. Detachment of Co. B, 2nd Dragoons. Soldiers wounded, 1.

December 20 .... Big Cypress Swamp, Fla. Detachment of Co. D, 4th U. S. Infty; and Co. I, 8th U. S. Infty. Soldiers killed,2; a Sergeant from the 8th Infty., and a private from the 4th Infty. Col. Wm. J. Worth commanded the expedition.

1842

January 25 .... Haw Creek, Fla. Branch of Wahoo Swamp. Cos. B, K, and a Detachment of Co. G, 2nd U. S. Infty. Major Joseph Plympton in command. Soldiers killed, 1. Soldiers wounded, 2. Indians captured, 2.

February 12 .... Wahoo Swamp, Fla. Co. H, 8th U. S. Infty. 1st Lieut. P. Smitsh in command. Soldiers killed, 1. Soldiers wounded, 1.

April 19 .... Big Hammock of Pilaklikaha, Fla. Co. K, 2nd Dragoons; Co. C, 2nd U. S. Infty; Cos. C, D, F, and I, 4th U. S. Infty.; Co. B, 8th U. S. Infty. Capt. Croghan Ker, 2nd Dragoons, in command. Soldiers killed, 1. Soldiers wounded, 3. All casualties in Co. K, 2nd Dragoons.

May 17 .... Ft. Wacahoota, Fla. Cos. D and E, 7th U. S. Infty. Soldiers killed, 2.

May 17 .... Near Clay's Landing, Suwannee River, Fla. Co. F, 7th U. S. Infty. 1st Lieut. F. Britton in command. Soldiers killed, 1. Soldiers wounded, 2.

1846

October 26—29, Between .... On Chihuahua Road out from Santa Fe, N. M. Detachment of Cos. G and I, 1st Dragoons. Skirmish with 70 Navajo Indians.

1847

June 26 .... Grand Prairie, near Arkansas River, Indian Territory. Co. B, 1st Dragoons. 1st Lieut. John Love in command. Soldiers killed, 5. Soldiers wounded, 6. Fight with Comanche Indians.

1848

February .... Vicinity of Los Angeles, Calif. Co. C, 1st Dragoons.

March .... 60 miles from Los Angeles, Calif. Co. C, 1st Dragoons. Skirmish with four Indians.

1849

March 13 .... El Cerro del Oya, N. M. Detachments of Cos. G, and I, 1st Dragoons. First Lieut. J. Whittesley in command. Soldiers killed, 2.

July 19 .... Canyon del Perron (Sierra Sacramento), N. M. Co. G, 1st Dragoons. Soldiers wounded, 1. Fight with the Apache Indians.

—9—

August 16 .... San Diego, crossing of the Rio Grande, near Dona Ana
    N. M. Company H, 1st Dragoons. Captain E. Steen in com-
    mand. Capt. Enoch Steen wounded. Soldiers wounded, 3.
    Fight with the Apache Indians.
October .... On the Little Blue River, near Linden, Nebr. Co. B, 1st
    Dragoons. Fight with Pawnee Indians.
October 29 .... Near Fort Kearny, on Platte River, Nebr. Detachment
    of Company B, 1st Dragoons. Captain R. H. Chilton in com-
    mand. Soldiers killed, 1. Fight was with the Pawnee In-
    dians.
November 17 ....Too Koon Kurre Butte, on Red River, N. M. Com-
    pany I, 1st Dragoons. Captain W. N. Grier in command.
    Soldiers wounded, 1. Fight was with Apache Indians.
November 21 ....Near Fort Lincoln, on Rio Saco, Texas. Detach-
    ment of Co. G, 2nd Dragoons. Capt. J. Oakes in command.
    Soldiers wounded, 1.

1850
February 2 .... Jornado del Muerto, N. M. Detachments of Co. H,
    1st dragoons.
February 20 .... Between Forts Inge and Duncan, Texas, Company E,
    8th U. S. Infty. Capt. J. T. Sprague in command. Soldiers
    killed, 1.
March 3 .... Chacon Creek, Texas. Detachment of Co. C, 2nd Dra-
    goons. Capt. W. J. Hardee in command. Soldiers killed, 1.
April 6 .... Near Rayado, N. M. Detachment of Co. I, 1st dragoons.
    Sergeant W. C. Holbrook in command. Indians killed, 5. In-
    dians wounded, 2. Sergeant and 10 men fought the Apache
    Indians.
April 7 .... Near Laredo, Texas. Companies G. and I., 1st U. S. In-
    fantry. Lieut. W. W. Hudson in command. Lieut. Hudson
    killed. Soldiers killed, 1. Soldiers wounded, 3.
May 19 .... Clear Lake and Pitt River, Calif. Co. C, 1st Dragoons;
    Detachments of Co. M, 3rd Artillery; and A. E. and G., 2nd
    U. S. Infty. Soldiers wounded, 2.
May 20 .... Frio Pass, near Leona, Texas. Detachments Co. C, 2nd
    Dragoons and Detachment Co. E, 8th U. S. Infty. Capt.
    Merchant, 8th Infty., in command. Capt. Merchant was
    wounded.
June 12 .... Near Laredo, Texas. Cos. H. and K., 1st U. S. Infty.
    Soldiers killed, 2. Soldiers wounded, 2.
July 5 .... Pitt River, Calif. Co. C, 1st Dragoons; Detachment of Co.
    M, 3rd Artillery; Detachment of Cos. A, E, and G, 2nd U. S.
    Inf. Soldiers killed, 1. Soldiers wounded, 1.
July 26 .... Headwaters of Canadian or Red River, N. M. Cos. G. and
    I., 1st Dragoons; and Co. K., 2nd Dragoons. Soldiers killed,
    1. Soldiers surprised a camp of 150 lodges. Lieut. John
    Adams, 1st Dragoons, in command.
August 12 .... Between Nueces and Rio Grande, Texas. Co. G., 2nd
    Dragoons. Capt. J. Oakes in command. Capt. Oakes was
    wounded.

1851
March 1 .... Near Ft. Atkinson, Nebr. Co. D, 6th U. S. Infty. Capt.

Wm. Hoffman in command. Soldiers killed, 1.

June 17 .... Near Rouge River, Oregon. Detachments of Cos. A. and E, 1st Dragoons. No details found.

June 25 .... On Sardine Creek, Calif. Detachment of Cos. A and E, 1st Dragoons.

August 26 .... Gila and Pinto Rivers, N. M. Detachments of Co. B, 1st dragoons. Lieut. A. Buford in command. Soldiers killed, 1. Soldiers wounded, 1. Indian killed, 1.

1852

January 24 to February 19 .... Near Laguna, on Jornado del Muerto, N. M. Cos. D, E, and K, 2nd Dragoons. Lieut. A. Pleasanton in command. Soldiers killed, 5.

February 6 .... Near Fort Webster, N. M. Co. K, 3rd U. S. Infty. Capt. I. B. Richardson in command. Soldiers killed, 3. Soldiers wounded, 1.

March 4   Below Yuma, Calif. Co. A, 1st Dragoons.

March 5 .... East Bank of Colorado River near Camp Yuma, Calif. Co. C, 1st Dragoons. Sergeant I. B. Taylor in command. Soldiers killed, 5.

July 4 .... Headwaters San Joaquin River, Calif. Co. B, 2nd U. S. Infty. First Lieut. T. Moore in command. Soldiers killed, 1.

August 25 .... Junction of Gila and Colorado Rivers, Calif. Company D, 2nd U. S. Infty. Capt. S. P. Heintzelman in command. Soldiers wounded, 2.

1853

March 24 .... Near the Red Bluffs, Calif. Co. D, 4th U. S. Infty. First Lieut. E. Russell in command. Lieut. Edmond Russell killed.

June 17 .... Near Ft. Laramie, Nebr. Co. G, 6th U. S. Infty. No details given.

August 24 .... Near Jacksonville, Ore. Detachment of Co. E, 4th U. S. Infty. Capt. B. R. Allen in command. Capt. Allen was wounded.

October 24 .... Near Illinois River, Ore. Cos. A., and E, 1st dragoons. Soldiers killed, 2.

October 26 .... Near Sevier Lake, Utah. Detachment of Co. A, mounted riflemen. No details given.

1854

March 5 .... Cangillon River, N. M. Co. H, 2nd Dragoons. Lieut. David Bell in command. Soldiers killed, 2. Soldiers wounded, 4. Fight was with the Iscarilla Indians under Lube.

March 12 .... Near Ft. Arbuckle, Indian Territory. Co. B, 2nd Dragoons. Lieut. A. B. Tree in command. Officers killed, 1. Soldiers killed, 1. Indians killed, 1. Lieut. Tree with 20 enlisted men captured and killed a Kickapoo Indian named "Thunder"—the murderer of Col. Stein and companion, March 12, 1854.

March 30 .... Cieneguilla, N. M. Co. I and Detachment of Co. F, 1st Dragoons. First Lieut. J. W. Davidson in command. Soldiers killed, 22—14 men of Co. I. and 8 men of Co. F. Fight was with the Apache Indians. Lieut. Davidson and 14 men wounded.

April 8 .... Ojo Caliente, N. M. Detachment of Co. I, 2nd Artillery; Co. H. and Detachment of Co. G, 1st Dragoons, and Co. H., 2nd Dragoons. Lieut. Col. Phillip Cooke in command. Soldiers killed, 1. Soldiers wounded, 1. Fight was with Apache Indians.

May 9 .... Lake Trinidad, Texas. Detachments of Cos. F. and I., mounted riflemen. Lieut. G. B. Cosby in command. Soldiers killed, 2. Lieut. Cosby wounded. 11 soldiers and 40 Indians took part in the fight.

June 30 .... South of Ft. Union, N. M. Company D, and Detachment of Co. H, 2nd Dragoons. Lieut. J. E. Maxwell killed by Apache Indians.

July 11 .... Near San Diego, Texas. Detachments of Cos. A. and H., Mounted Riflemen. Captain VanBuren in command. Capt. Van Buren wounded. Soldiers wounded, 2. Fight was between 16 soldiers and the Comanche Indians.

August 19 .... Near Fort Laramie, Nebr. Co. G, 6th U. S. Infty. Lieut. J. L. Grattan in command. Lieut. Grattan and 29 soldiers killed by the Sioux Indians

August 28 .... Attack on Ft. Laramie, Nebr., Co. G., 6th U. S. Infty. No details given.

September 5 .... The Lobo, near Rio Grande, Texas. Detachment of Co. D, Mounted Riflemen. Capt. D. Jones in command. Soldiers killed, 1.

October 3 .... Ft. Davis, near the Limpia, Texas. Detachments of Co. D., and K., Mounted Riflemen. No details given.

October 11 .... Live Oak, Texas. Co. F, 1st U. S. Infty. Capt. B. H. Arthur in command. Indians killed, 2.

November 1 .... Near Fort Davis, Texas Co. G., 8th U. S. Infty. First Lieut. Theo. Fink in command. Soldiers killed, 3.

1855

January 7 .... Pecos River, Texas. Co. A. and Detachment of Co. G., Mounted Riflemen. Capt. W. L. Elliott in command. Several Comanche Indians were killed.

January 15 .... White Mountains, South-east of Los Lunas, N. M. Detachment of Co. H, 1st Dragoons. Capt. J. H. Whittlesey in command. Soldiers killed, 1.

January 17 .... Camp on Pensaco River, N. M. Cos. B, G, and Detachment of Co. K, 1st Dragoons.

January 18 .... On Penasco River, N. M., while on the march. Cos. B, G, and Detachment of Co. K, 1st Dragoons.

January 19 .... Penasco River, N. M. Co. B, 1st Dragoons. Capt. H. W. Stanton in command. Capt. Stanton killed by Apache Indians. Soldiers killed, 2.

February 24 .... White Mountains, southeast of Los Lunas, N. M. Detachment of Co. G., 1st Dragoons. Capt. R. S. Ewell in command. Soldiers killed, 2.

March 19 .... Cochotope Pass, N. M. Cos. D. and F., 1st Dragoons; Co. D., 2nd Artillery. Capt. H. Brooks, 2nd Artillery, in command. Soldiers wounded, 2. 100 Apache and Utah Indians met Col. Fauntleroy's command.

March 21—23 .... Puncha Pass, Arkansas River, N. M., Cos. D, and F., 1st Dragoons; Co. D, 2nd Artillery. Capt. H. Brooks, 2nd Artillery, in command. Soldiers wounded, 1.

April 25 .... Crossing of Huerfano River, (Colo.) N. M. Co. F, 1st Dragoons.

April 29 .... Near Headwaters of Arkansas River, N. M., Co. D., 1st Dragoons; Co. D., 2nd Artillery. Capt. H. Brooks in command. Soldiers killed, 1. Soldiers wounded, 2. Indians killed, 50. The Utah and Apache Indians fought Col. Fauntleroy's command.

May 1—2 .... Chowatch Valley, N. M. Co. D, 1st Dragoons; Co. D., 2nd Artillery. No details given.

June 13 .... Near Junction Delaware Creek and Pecos River, N. M. Co. I, 5th U. S. Infty. Capt. C. L. Stevenson in command. Soldiers killed, 4.

July 22 .... Vicinity of Eagle Springs, Texas. Detachment of Co. I, Mounted Riflemen. Capt. C. F. Ruff in command. Indians killed, 13. Fight with Mescalero Indians.

September 3 .... Blue Water or Ash Hollow, Nebr. Cos. E. and K., 2nd Dragoons; Co. G, 4th Artillery; Cos. A., E, H, I., K., 6th U. S. Infty; and Co. E, 10th U. S. Infty. Gen. W. S. Harney and Major A. Cady in command. Soldiers killed, 7. Soldiers wounded, 5. Indians killed, 22. Indians captured, 35. Fight was with Sioux Indians.

October 6—9 .... Topinish, Simcoe Valley, Oregon. Cos. I. and K., Detachment of Co. H., 4th U. S. Infty. Capt. G. O. Haller in command. Soldiers killed, 5. Soldiers wounded, 17. 1500 Yakima warriors toop part in the fight.

October 25 .... Between Grave and Cow Creek, Ore. Detachment of Co. H., 3rd Artillery. Lieut. J. Dayadale in command. Soldiers killed, 2. One Sergeant, one Corporal, and 10 privates were attacked by Rogue River Indians.

October 31 to November 1 .... Hungry Hill, between Grave and Cow Creeks, Oregon. Co. E and detachment of Co. C., 1st Dragoons; Detachments of Cos. D. and H., 3rd Artillery; Detachments of Cos. D. and E., 4th U. S. Infty. Capt. A. L. Smith, 1st Dragoons, and Capt. Jackson in command. Lieut. H. S. Gibson wounded. Soldiers killed and wounded, 26. Battle with Rogue River Indians.

November 4—5 .... White River, Washington Territory. Cos. A. and C.. 4th U. S. Infty. First Lieut. W. H. Slaughter in command. Soldiers killed, 1. Citizens killed, 19.

November 6—7 .... Puyallup River, Washington Territory. Cos. A. and C., 4th U. S. Infty. First Lieut. W. A. Slaughter in command. Soldiers killed, 2. Soldiers wounded, 2. Battle with Rouge River Indians.

November 9 .... Two Buttes, on Yakima River, Ore. Cos. G and I, 4th U. S. Infty. The Indians presented a show of force, hollered and exchanged shots with the soldiers, but made no attack, and when the troops advanced the Indians fled. Only one fatality—an unarmed Indian mounted on a slow horse was overtaken and killed by an Indian Scout. Major Gabriel J. Rains was in command.

December 4 .... Brannan's Prairie, Washington Territory. Detachment of Co. M., 3rd Artillery; Co. C. and Detachment of Co. A., 4th U. S. Infty. First Lieut. W. A. Slaughter in command. Lieut. W. A. Slaughter, 4th Infty., killed. Soldiers killed, 1. Soldiers wounded, 3.

December 20 .... Billy's Town, near Fort Myers, Florida. Detachments of Cos. E., G., and K., (10 men) 2nd Artillery. Lieut. G. L. Hartsuff in command. Soldiers killed, 4. Lieut. G. L. Hartsuff wounded. Soldiers wounded, 3.

1856

January 18 .... Near Fort Deynaud, Fla. Detachments of Cos. C. and L., 2nd Artillery. Corporal Wm. Love in command. Soldiers killed, 5. Soldiers wounded, 1. 6 soldiers were attacked by Seminole Indians.

February 22 .... Headwaters Nueces, Texas. Co. C., 2nd Cav. Capt. James Oakes in command. Soldiers wounded, 2.

March 1 .... White River near Muckleshute Prairie, Washington Territory. Detachment of Co. M., 3rd Artillery; Co. A., 4th U. S. Infty. Cos. D. and H., 9th U. S. Infty. Colonel Casey and Capt. E. D. Keyes in command. Soldiers killed, 1. Lieut. Kautz wounded. Soldiers wounded, 6. 26 men went to the relief of Lieut. Kautz.

March 8 .... Guadalupe River, Texas. Detachment of Co. I., 2nd U. S. Cav. Details not given.

March 20 .... Almagre Mountains, near Ft. Thorn, N. M. Cos. G K., and detachment of D., 1st Dragoons; Cos. D., F., and I., 3rd U. S. Infty. Capt. D. J. Chandler and Lieut. I. N. Moore in command. Soldiers wounded, 1. Fight with the Mogollon Apaches.

March 20 .... Mouth of Rogue River, Oregon. Co. B., 3rd Artillery Capt. E. O. C. Ord in command. Soldiers wounded, 2. Indians killed, 8. Indians wounded, 8.

March 21 .... Near Ft. McIntosh, Texas. Detachment of Co. F., 1st Artillery. First Lieut, J. E. Slaughter in command. Indians wounded, 2.

March 21 .... Almagre Mountains, N. M. Co. B. and I., 3rd U. S. Infty. No details given.

March 22 .... Illinois River, Oregon. Co. C., 1st Dragoons; Detachment of Co. E., 4th U. S. Infty. Capt. A. J. Smith is in command. Soldiers killed, 2. Soldiers wounded, 4. Fight with Rogue River Indians.

March 26 .... Cascades of Columbia River, Washington Territory. Co. H., 4th U. S. Infty. Capt. H. D. Wallen in command. Soldiers killed, 1. Soldiers wounded, 2. One Sergeant and 8 Privates attacked at Block House

March 26 .... Mackanootney Village, Oregon. Co. B., 3rd U. S. Artillery; and Co. F., 4th U. S. Infty. Capt. E. O. C. Ord in command. Soldiers wounded, 1.

March 27—28 .... Cascades of Columbia River, Washington Territory. Detachment of Co. E., 1st Dragoons; Co. L., 3rd Artillery; Cos. A., E., F., and I., 9th U. S. Infty. Col. Wright, 9th Infty, and First Lieut. Alex Piper, 3rd Artillery, in command. Soldiers killed, 2. Soldiers wounded, 2. Indians killed, 3.

March 28 ...... Mimbres River, N. M. Cos. G, I, K, and Detachment of Co. D, 1st Dragoons.

March 29 .... Near Chocoliska, Fla. Cos. E. and G., 2nd Artillery. Capt. Arnold Elzey in command. Soldiers killed, 2. Soldiers wounded, 1. Fight with Seminoles.

March 29 ...... Mimbres Mountains, N. M. Cos. B. and I., 3rd U. S. Infty. No details given.

April 6—7 ...... Big Cypress Swamp, near Billy's Town, Fla. Co. L., 1st. Artillery; Cos. C., and L., 2nd Artillery. Capt. L. G. Arnold in command. Soldiers killed, 1. Soldiers wounded, 3. Fight with Seminoles.

April 13 ...... Turkey Branch, Headwaters of the Nueces, Texas. Cos. B. and D., Mounted Riflemen; and Co. F., 1st Artillery. Capt. T. Claiborne in command. Indians killed, 1. Indians wounded, 1. Indians captured, 4.

April 25 ...... Cedar Creek, Washington Territory. Co. K. 9th U. S. Infty. Capt. F. T. Dent in command. Soldiers wounded, 1.

April 29 ...... Chetoo River, Oregon. Co. B., 3rd Artillery. Capt. E. O. C. Ord in command. Soldiers wounded, 1. Indians killed, 2. Indians wounded, 3. Several Checto Indians captured.

Early May ...... Mouth of Hood River, Ore. Co. E, 1st Dragoons.

May 1 ...... Headwaters of the Concho River, Texas. Detachment of Co. C., 2nd U. S. Cav. Capt. James Oakes in command. Indians killed, 1.

May 1—9 ...... Headwaters Nasquelly River, Washington Territory. Detachment of Co. H., 9th U. S. Infty. Second Lieut. D. B. McKibbin in command. Indians killed, 3. Indians captured 16.

May 27 ...... Devil's River, near Ft. Clark, Texas. Detachment of Cos. C., H., Mounted Riflemen. Capt. A. J. Lindsay in command Soldiers wounded, 1.

May 27—28 ...... Big Bend of Rogue River, Oregon. Co. C. 1st Dragoons, Co. G. and Detachment of Co. E., 4th U. S. Infty. Col. Buchanan in command. Soldiers killed, 9. Soldiers wounded, 3.

June ...... Several slight skirmishes in Oregon. Co. E, 1st Dragoons.

July 1 ...... Source of Colo. and Brazos River, Texas. Co. A., 2nd U. S. Cav. Lieut. E. VanDorn in command. Indians killed, 2. Indians wounded, 1.

August 2 ...... Punta Rassa, Fla. Co. E., 2nd Artillery. First Lieut. H. Benson in command. Soldiers killed, 1. Fight was with the Seminoles.

August 30—September 8 .... Junction of Rio Grande and Pecos Rivers, Texas. Detachment of Co. C. 2nd Cav.; Detachment of Co. I., 1st Artillery; Detachment of Co. B., 1st U. S. Infty.

November 18 ...... Concho River, Texas. Detachment of Co. G., 2nd U. S. Cav., Capt. W. R. Bradfute in command. Soldiers wounded, 1.

November 26 .... Concho River, Texas. Detachment of Co. G., 2nd U. S. Cav. Capt. W. A. Bradfute in command. Soldiers wounded, 1. Indians killed, 4. Indians captured, 1. Fight with Comanche Indians.

November 30 .... Near Sacramento Mountains, N. M. Detachment of Co. C. Mounted Riflemen and Co. G., 1st Dragoons.

December 18 .... Near Fort Clark, on Rio Grande, Texas. Detachment of Co. C., 2nd Cav., Lieut. J. B. Witherell in command. Indians killed, 2.

December 21 .... Near Ft. Clark, Texas. Detachment of Co. C., 2nd U. S. Cav.

December 22 .... Headwaters of Main Concho River, Texas. Detachment of Co. F., 2nd U. S. Cav. Lieut. R. W. Johnson in command. Soldiers killed, 2. Soldiers wounded, 2. Indians killed, 3. Indians wounded, 3. Fight with Comanche Indians.

1857

January 31 .... Howard Springs, near Ft. Lancaster, Texas. Detachments of Cos. A., C., F., G., and H., 8th U. S. Infty. Soldiers killed, 4.

February 12 .... On North Branch of Concho River, Texas. Detachment of Co. B., 2nd U. S. Cav.

February 13 .... Kickapoo Creek, near Concho River, Texas. Detachment of Co. D., 2nd U. S. Cav.

March 4—April 23 .... Big Cypress Swamp, Fla. Co. M., 4th Artillery; Cos. A, B, D., E., F., G., H., and I., 5th U. S. Infty. Capt. Brown (and others) in command. Soldiers killed, 12. Lieut. Freeman wounded. Soldiers wounded, 6.

March 9 .... Northern Slope of Sierra de los Mimbres, N. M. Detachment of Co. G., Mounted Riflemen. First Lieut. A. Gibbs in command, who was wounded. Indians killed, 6. Indians wounded, 1.

March 11 .... Ojo del Muerto, N. M. Detachment of Co. B., Mounted Riflemen. Lieut. L. S. Baker in command. Soldiers killed, 2. Soldiers wounded, 4. Indians killed, 7. Indians wounded, 4. One Officer and 35 soldiers fought the Apache Indians.

April 4 .... Headwaters North Branch of Nueces River, Texas. Detachment of Co. B., 2nd U. S. Cav.

April 19 .... Headwaters of the Nueces River, Texas. Detachment of Co. B., 2nd U. S. Cav.

May 24 .... Mogollon Mountains, El Canyon de los Muertos (Carneros), N. M. Cos. C., D., and I., Mounted Riflemen; Co. B. and Detachment of Co. F., 3rd U. S. Infty. Lieut. Col. G. B. Crittenden in command. Indians killed, 7. Indians captured, 9. Gila Expedition.

June 10 .... Pitt River Canyon, Calif. Co. D., 4th Infty. 1st. Lieut. Geo. Crook in command. Lieut. Crook wounded by an arrow.

June 27 .... Gila River, N. M. Cos. B. and G., and Detachment of Co. D., 1st Dragoons; Cos. B., G., and K, 3rd Infty.; Cos. B., H., and I., 8th U. S. Infty. Colonel Loring and Capt. T. Clayborne in command. Lieut. A. E. Steen wounded. Soldiers wounded, 3. Gila Expedition against Coyolero Apaches.

June 30 .... Headwaters Rio Frio, Texas. Detachment of Co. B., 2nd U. S. Cav.

July 2 .... South Branch of Llano River, Texas. Detachment of Co. B., 2nd U. S. Cav.

July 2 to July 26 .... Pitt River Country, Calif. Co. D., 4th U. S. Infty.

July 20 .... Headwaters of Devil's River, Texas. Detachment of Co. G., 2nd U. S. Cav.

July 24 .... Pecos River, near Ft. Lancaster, Texas. Detachments of Cos. H. and K., 1st U. S. Infty; Detachments of Cos. C., D., F., and H., 8th U. S. Infty.

July 29 .... Solomon's Fork, Kansas River, Kansas. Cos. A., B., D., E., G., and H., 1st Cavalry; Cos. C., D., and G., 6th Infantry. Col. E. V. Sumner in command. Soldiers killed, 1. Lieut. J. E. B. Stuart wounded. Soldiers wounded, 8. Indians killed, 10. Indians wounded, 10. Cheyenne Expedition—400 Indians.

August 5—12 .... Fort Crook, Calif. Detachment of Co. A., 1st Dragoons; Co. D., 4th U. S. Infty. Captain H. L. Scott in command. Soldiers wounded, 1. Fight with Pitt River Indians.

August 10 .... Wichita Mountains, Indian Territory. Detachments of Cos. C. and K., 2nd U. S. Cav. No other details given.

September 24 .... Headwaters of the Brazos, Texas. Co. H., 2nd U. S. Cav. No details.

September 25 .... Santa Caterina, Texas. Detachment of Co. I, 2nd U. S. Cav. No details.

October 12 .... Salamonana, Texas. Co. I, 2nd U. S. Cav. No details.

October 30 .... Verde River, Texas. Co. D., 2nd U. S. Cav. No details.

November 8 .... Head of West Branch of Nueces River, Texas. Detachments of Cos. C. and K., 2nd Cav. No details.

December 7 .... Ladrone Mountains, Ft. Craig, N. M. Detachments of Co. F., Mounted Riflemen. Lieut. W. W. Overall in command. Indians killed, 5. Indians captured, 1. 11 soldiers fought with 6 Kiowa Indians.

December 13 .... Dragoons Springs, N. M. Detachment of Co. F., Mounted Riflemen. No details.

1858

January 28 .... South Branch of Llano River, Texas. Detachment of Co. D., 2nd U. S. Cav. Capt. I. N. Palmer in command. Soldiers wounded, 3.

March 11 .... Huachuca Mountains, N. M. Detachment of Co. G., 1st Dragoons. First Lieut. I. N. Moore in command. Lieut. Moore was wounded. Indian killed, 1. 30 soldiers fought a band of Apaches.

April 21 .... Near Fort Scott, Kans. Cos. C. and I., 1st U. S. Cav. Capt. Geo. Anderson in command. Soldiers killed, 1.

May 17 .... To-ho-to-nim-me, near Spokane Lake, Washington Territory. Cos. C., E., and H., 1st Dragoons; Detachment of Co. D., 9th Infty. (25 men). Lieut. Col. Steptoe in command. Capt. O. H. P. Taylor and Lieut. Wm. Gaston killed. Soldiers killed, 6. Soldiers wounded, 3. 800 to 1000 Spokane and other Indians engaged in battle.

May 30 .... Ewell's Hay Camp, near Ft. Defiance, N. M. Detachment of Co. I., Mounted Riflemen; Cos. B., and G., 3rd U. S. Infty. No details.

June 16 .... Near Guadalupe Mountains, Texas. Detachments of Cos. C., D., F., and H., 8th U. S. Infty. No details.

August 15 .... Yakima River, Washington Territory. Cos. C., G., and I., 9th U. S. Infty. Major R. S. Garnett in command. Second Lieut. J. K. Allen killed.

August 29 .... Near Bear Springs, N. M. Detachment of Co. I., Mounted Riflemen. Capt. G. McLane in command. Capt. McLane wounded. Indians killed, 10. Indians wounded, 4. Indians captured, 4. 12 soldiers, 22 Mexicans, and 300 Navajoes took part in the battle.

September 1—5, 8 .... Four Lakes and Spokane Plains, Washington Territory. Cos. C., E., H., I., and Detachment of Co. D., 1st Dragoons; Cos. A., B., G., K., and M., 3rd Artillery; Cos. B. and F., 9th U. S. Infty. Col. Geo. Wright in command. Soldiers wounded, 1.

September 9 to 15 .... Operations from Fort Defiance, N. M. Cos. A., F., H., and I., Mounted Riflemen; Cos. B., C., 3rd U. S. Infty. Col. D. S. Miles and D. S. Loring in command. Soldiers killed, 2. Soldiers wounded, 3. Fight with the Navajoes.

September 10 .... Okanogan River, Washington Territory. Cos. C., G. and I., 9th U. S. Infty. Capts. J. W. Frazer, H. M. Black, and J. J. Archer in command. Soldiers killed, 1.

September 19—24 .... Canyon de Chelly, near Ft. Defiance, N. M., Co. G., 3rd U. S. Infty. Capt. T. H. Brooks in command. Indians killed, 6. Indians wounded, 1.

September 25 .... Laguna Negro, N. M. Co. I., Mounted Riflemen; Co. D., 3rd U. S. Infty. No details.

September 28—29 .... Chusca Valley and Mountains, N. M. Detachment of Co. E., Mounted Riflemen, Co. K., 8th U. S. Infty. Capt. T. Duncan in command. Indians killed, 2. Indian wounded, 4.

October 1 .... Bear Springs, N. M. Cos. A., F., H., I., Mounted Riflemen; Co. B., 3rd U. S. Infty. Capt. Andrew J. Lindsey in command. Soldiers killed, 2. Soldiers wounded, 1. Indians killed, 8. Many Indians wounded.

October 1 .... Near Wichita Village, Choctaw Nation, Indian Territory. Cos. A., F., H., and K., 2nd Cav. Major Earl Van Dorn in command. Lieut. C. Van Camp killed. Major E. Van Dorn wounded. Soldiers killed, 3. Soldiers wounded 10. Indians killed, 56. Fight with Comanches.

October 2 .... Laguna Chusca, near Fort Defiance, N. M. Cos. A. and C., Mounted Riflemen. Capt. W. L. Elliott in command. Soldiers killed, 1. Soldiers wounded, 1. Fought Navajoe Indians.

October 6 .... San Juan River, N. M. Cos. B. and E., 8th U. S. Infty. No details.

October 9 .... Rio Puerco of the West, N. M. Cos. F. and H., Mounted Riflemen. Capt. A. J. Lindsay in command. Lieut. Overall wounded. Many Indians killed and wounded.

October 10 .... Ojo del Oso, N. M. Detachment of Co. A., Mounted
Riflemen; Detachment of Co. G., 3rd U. S. Infty; Detachment of Co. K., 8th U. S. Infty. Capt. W. L. Elliott, Co. A.,
Mounted Riflemen, and Major Brooks in command. Soldiers
wounded, 2. Many of the 150 Navajoe Indians were killed
and wounded.

October 17 .... Canyon Bonita, N. M. Co. I., Mounted Riflemen. Capt.
Geo. McLane in command. Soldiers killed, 1. Soldiers
wounded, 5. Indians killed, 3. 200 Navajo Indians attacked
Herd Guard.

October 18 .... Juan Chu Mountains, N. M. Cos. F., H., and I.,
Mounted Riflemen. Capt. A. J. Lindsay in command. Indians killed, 1.

October 19 to November 18 .... Navajo Expedition, N. M. Cos. E.
and G., Mounted Riflemen; Co. D., 3rd U. S. Infty.; Cos. B.,
E., and I., 8th U. S. Infty. Soldiers wounded, 2. Indians killed,
1. Fight with Zuni Indian Scouts.

November 1 .... Canon de Chelly, N. M. Co. H., Mounted Riflemen.
Capt. A. J. Lindsay in command. Soldiers wounded, 1.

November 9 .... Near Carrizo, N. M. Co. F., 3rd Infty. No details.

1859

January 9 .... Mojave Country, Calif. Detachments of Cos. B. and
K., 1st Dragoons. Major William Hoffman, 6th Infty., in
command. Indians killed, 18. There were 27 soldiers from
Co. B. and 25 from Co. K., against 300 Mojave and Painte
Indians.

February 8 .... Dog Canyon (Sacramento Mts.) N. M. Detachment of
Co. D., Mounted Riflemen. Lieut. H. M. Lazelle (8th Infty.)
in command. Soldiers killed, 3. Soldiers wounded, 8.

February 13 .... Near Ft. Inge, Texas. Detachment of Co. F., 8th
U. S. Infty. No details.

February 24 .... Caddo Creek, near Ft. Arbuckle, Choctaw Nation,
Indian Territory. Detachments of Cos. D. and E., 1st U. S.
Cav., Detachment of Co. E., 1st U. S. Infty. 1st Lieut. J. E.
Powell, 1st Infty., in command. Soldiers killed, 1. Soldiers
wounded, 2.

February 27—28 .... Caddo Creek, near Ft. Arbuckle, Choctaw Nation, Indian Territory. Detachment of Co. D., 1st U. S. Cav.
Capt. J.McIntosh in command. Indians killed, 7. Fight
with Comanche Indians.

April 27 .... Near Ft. Fillmore, N. M. Co. D., 1st Dragoons. No
details.

May 2 .... Great Comanche Trail, Texas. Co. I., 2nd U. S. Cav. Capt.
A. G. Brackett in command. Indians killed, 2. Indians
wounded, 1. Fight with Comanche Indians.

May 13 .... Nescutunga Valley, 15 miles south of old Ft. Atkinson,
Texas. Cos. A, B, C., F., G., and H., 2nd U. S. Cav. Capt.
E. K. Smith in command. Soldiers killed, 2. Capt. E. K.
Smith and 2nd Lieut. F. Lee wounded. Soldiers wounded,
13. Indians killed, 49. Indians wounded, 5. Indians cap-
tured, 36. Battle with Comanche Indians.

May 20 .... Near Ft. Inge, Texas. Detachment of Co. F., 8th Infty. No details.

August .... Near Salmon Falls, Wash. Ter. Co. E, and Detachment of Co. H, 1st Dragoons. Fight with Snake Indians.

August 5 .... Near Fort Mojave, N. M. Detachments of Cos. F. and I., 8th U. S. Infty. Capt. L. A. Armistead in command. Soldiers wounded, 3. Indians killed, 23. 2 officers and 50 soldiers against 200 Mojave Indians.

August 13 .... Devil's Gate Canyon, near Box Elder, Utah. Co. G., 2nd Dragoons. Lieut. Ebenezer Gay in command. Soldiers wounded, 6.

August 14 .... Box Elder, Ind. Ter. Co. E, and Detachment of Co. H, 1st Dragoons. Fight with Bannock Indians.

August 15 .... Hat Creek Station, Calif. Detachment of Co. F, 1st Dragoons. Fight with Apaches.

October 18 .... Near Jemez, 60 miles from Cantonment Burgwin, N. M. Detachment of Co. E., Mounted Riflemen.

October 30 .... Near Pawnee Fork, Kans. Detachment of Co. K., 1st U. S. Cav. First Lieut. David Bell in command. Indians killed, 2. 23 soldiers against a band of Kiowa Indians.

November 3 .... Headwaters of the Llano, Texas. Detachment of Co. F., 8th U. S. Infty. No details.

November 12—26 .... Pinal Apache Expedition, N. M. Co. D. and Detachment of Co. G., 1st Dragoons; Co. A. and Detachment of Co. D. and H., Mounted Riflemen. Capt. I. V. D. Reeve 8th Infty., in command. Indians captured, 22

November 14 .... Tunicha, N. M. Detachments of Cos. B., C., E., and G., 3rd U. S. Infty. Capt. O. L. Shepherd in command. Indians killed, 2. Indians wounded, 6. Tuni Chay Apaches in fight.

December 3 .... Santa Teresa Mountains, N. M. Detachment of Co. A., Mounted Riflemen. 2nd Lieut. H. C. McNeill in command. Indians killed, 2. Indians wounded, 3.

December 4 .... Mail Escort, Ft. Union, N. M. Detachment of Co. H., Mounted Riflemen. Sergeant F. M. Cabe in command. Indians killed, 2. Fight with Kiowa Indians.

December 13—14 .... The Ebonel, near Brownsville, Texas. Co. E., 2nd Cav., Cos. C., L., and M., 1st Artillery. No details.

December 14 .... On North Branch of Guadalupe River, Texas. Detachment of Co. I., 2nd U. S. Cav. No details.

December 14 .... East of Ft. Buchanan, N. M. Cos. D. and G., 1st Dragoons. Fight with Apaches.

December 18 .... Santa Teresa Mountains, N. M. Detachment A., Mounted Riflemen. Capt. W. L. Elliott in command. Indians killed, 2. Indians wounded, 4.

December 24 .... Pinal Co., Pinal Mts., Ariz. Co. G., 1st Dragoons. Capt. R. S. Ewell in command. Indians killed, 6. Fought Apaches.

December 27 .... Ringgold Barracks, Rio Grande City, Texas. Co. E., 2nd U. S. Cav.; Cos. C., L., M., 1st Artillery. Soldiers killed, 1. Soldiers wounded, 1. Cortina Troubles.

1860

January 16 .... Pecan Bayou, near Camp Colorado, Texas. Detachment of Co. B, 2nd U. S. Cavalry. Lieut F. Lee in command. Indians killed, 2.

January 17 .... Near Ft. Defiance, N. M. Detachments of Cos. B, C, E, and G, 3rd U. S. Infty. Soldiers killed, 4. Battle between a cattle guard of 35 soldiers and 250 Navajoe Indians.

January 18—22 .... Bacon Springs, near Fort Defiance, N. M. Detachments of Troops B, C, E, F, G, 3rd U. S. Infty. Corporal Edgar in command. Soldiers killed, 1, Fight with Navajoes.

January 26 .... Kickapoo Creek, Texas. Detachment of Co. A, 2nd U. S. Cavalry. Major Geo. H. Thomas in command. Indians killed, 4. Fight with the Comanche Indians.

January 30 .... Aqua Frio, Texas. Detachment of Co. C, 2nd U. S. Cavalry. No details given.

February 7 .... Canyon Alamosa, N. M. Detachment of Co. F, Mounted Riflemen. First Sergeant McQuade in command. Indians killed, 2.

February 8 .... Near Fort Defiance, N. M. Detachments of Cos. B, C, E, G, 3rd U. S. Infty. Sergt. Werner, Co. C, in command. Soldiers wounded, 1. Fight between 44 soldiers and 500 Navajoe Indians.

February 8 .... Canyon del Muerto, N. M. Cos. F. and I, Mounted Riflemen. Capt. A. Porter in command. Indians killed, 6. Indians wounded, 5.

February 8 .... Canyon del Muerto, N. M. Co. I, Mounted Riflemen. Capt. Geo. McLane in command. Indian killed, 15.

February 13 .... Between Kickapoo and Brady Creek, near Ft. Mason, Ark. Co. F, 2nd U. S. Cavalry. Capt. R. W. Johnson in command. Indians killed, 1. Indians wounded, 2.

April 5 .... Near Ft. Defiance, N. M. Detachment of Co. B, 3rd U. S. Infty. No details given.

April 18 .... Near Camp Cady on Mojave River, Calif. Cos. B and K, 1st Dragoons. Capt. J. H. Carleton in command. Soldiers wounded, 3. Indians killed, 2. Pah-Ute Indians in fight.

April 19 .... Near Camp Cady, on the Mojave River, Calif. Cos. B and K, 1st Dragoons. Skirmish with Pah-Ute Indians.

April 30 .... Attack on Ft. Defiance, N. M. Cos. B, C, and E, 3rd U. S. Infty. Maj. O. L. Shepherd in command. Soldiers killed, 1. Soldiers wounded, 2. Fight with Navajoe Indians.

May 2 .... Near Providence Mts., Ariz. Detachments Cos. B. and K. 1st Dragoons. Lieut. M. T. Carr in command. Indians killed, 3. Indians wounded, 1. Indians captured, 1. Pah-Ute Indians in engagement.

May 7 .... Near Ft. Lancaster, Texas. Co. K, 1st U. S. Infty. No details given.

June 2 .... Truckee River near Pyramid Lake, Nevada. Detachments of Cos. A. and F., 1st Dragoons; Co. H. and Detachments of Cos. I. and M., 3rd U. S. Artillery; Cos. A. and H., 6th U. S. Infty. Capt. J. Stewart in command. Soldiers wounded, 4.

June 23 .... Near Harney Lake, Oregon. Co. C, 1st Dragoons. Capt. A. J. Smith in command. Indians killed, 1. Fight with Snake Indians.

July 11 .... Blackwater Springs, near Bent's Ford, Nebr. Detachments of Cos. F, G, H, and K, 1st Cav. Detachments of Cos. C. and K, 2nd Dragoons. Major J. Sedgwick in command. Lieut. G. D. Bayard, 1st Cav., wounded. Soldiers wounded, 2.

July 15 .... Canada de los Penavetitos, N. M. Cos. A, C, D, F, H, and K, Mounted Riflemen. No details given.

July 23 .... Hatch's Ranch, N. M. Co. E, 8th U. S. Infty. No details given.

August 2 .... Near Albuquerque, N. M. Detachment of Co. I, Mounted Riflemen. Lieut. D. C. Stith in command. Indians killed, 2. Indians captured, 2. Fight with Navajoe Indians.

August 6 .... Cottonwood Creek, Kansas. Cos. A, B, C, D, E, and I, 1st U. S. Cavalry. Major John Sedgwick in command. Soldiers wounded, 1. Kiowa and Comanche Indians in engagement.

August 11 .... Eagan Canyon and Deep Creek, Utah. Company B, 4th U. S. Artillery. 1st Lieut. S. H. Weed in command. Soldiers wounded, 3. Indians killed, 1.

August 26 .... Near Ft. Buchanan, N. M. Co. D, 1st Dragoons. Lieut. D. H. Hastings in command. Indians killed, 1. Fight with Apaches.

August 26—27 .... Near the Head of Clear Fork, Brazos River, Texas. Band, Co. B, and Detachment of Co. B, 2nd U. S. Cavalry. Major G. H. Thomas in command. Soldiers killed 1. Major Thomas wounded. Soldiers wounded, 4. Indians killed, 1. Indians wounded, 2.

September 6 .... Deep Creek, Utah. Detachment of Co. B, 4th U. S. Artillery. Capt. John Gibbon in command. Soldiers wounded, 1.

September 18 .... Ft. Fauntleroy, N. M. Detachments of Cos. C, D, and H, 5th U. S. Infty. Herd Guards. Soldiers wounded, 5. Indians killed, 10. 40 Indians attacked Herd Guard.

September 23 .... Navajo Country, N. M. Co. I, Mounted Riflemen. Capt. G. McLane in command. Indians wounded, 1.

September 24 .... Near Fort Fauntleroy, N. M. Detachment of Co. E, 7th U. S. Infty. Capt. H. Little in command. Soldiers wounded, 1.

September 26 .... Near Fort Fauntleroy, N. M. Detachment of Co. K, 7th U. S. Infty. 1st Lieut. A. H. Plummer in command. Soldiers wounded, 1.

October 3 .... Tunicha Mountains, near Sierra de los Estrellos, N. M. Co. A, 10th U. S. Infty. Capt. A. D. Nelson in command. Soldiers wounded, 1. Indians killed, 10. Indians captured, 5. Fight with Navajo Indians.

October 3 .... Chaparita, N. M. Co. K, 8th U. S. Infty. Capt. E. B. Hollaway in command. Indians killed, 2. Fight with Comanche Indians.

October 13—28 .... South Base of Black Rock, near Cold Springs, Navajo Country, N. M. Cos. B and I, Mounted Riflemen;

Cos. G and I, 2nd Dragoons; Cos. A, B, D, F, G, and I, 5th
U. S. Infty; Co. K, 7th U. S. Infty.; Co. A, 10th U. S. Infty.
Capt. Thos. Clayborne, Jr., in command. Capt. G. McLane
killed. Indians killed, 7. Indians captured, 8. Indians
wounded, 1. Fight with Navajo Indians.

October 24 .... San Jose, N. M. Cos. B and I, Mounted Riflemen.
Capt. Thomas Claiborne in command. Indians killed, 3. Indians captured, 5. Fight with Navajo Indians.

November 19 .... Los Calitas, N. M. Co. A, 5th U. S. Infty.; Cos. D
and K, 7th U. S. Infty. No details given.

December 19 .... Pease River, Texas. Detachment of Co. H, 2nd
U. S. Cavalry. First Sergt. J. W. Spangler in command. Indians killed, 14. Indians captured, 3. 25 Comanche Indians in the fight.

1861

January 2 .... Near Cold Spring on the Cimarron River, N. M. Cos.
D, H, K and detachment of Co. E, Mounted Riflemen. Lieut.
Col. G. B. Crittenden in command. Soldiers wounded, 3.
Indians killed, 10. Fight with Kiowa and Comanche Indians.

January 3 .... Chusca Valley, N. M. Co. K, 5th U. S. Infty. Capt.
N. B. Rossell in command. Soldiers fight with Navajo Indians.

January 7 .... Near Ft. Fauntleroy, N. M. Co. G, 5th U. S. Infty.;
Co. A, 10th U. S. Infty. 1st Lieut. W. H. Lewis in command.
Indians killed, 4. Indians captured, 17.

February 4—19 .... Apache Pass, N. M. Co. C. 7th U. S. Infty. 2nd
Lieut. G. N. Bascom in command. Soldiers wounded, 2. Indians captured, 9.

February 14 .... Apache Pass, Ariz. T. Co. D, 1st Dragoons. No details given.

April 14—15 .... Mad River, Calif. Detachment Co. B, 6th U. S.
Infty. Lieut. J. B. Collins, 4th U. S. Infty., in command. Soldiers wounded, 1. Indians killed, 25. Indians wounded, 3.

May 8 .... Redwood Creek, Calif. Detachment of Co. B, 4th U. S.
Infty., Sergt. Hartman in command. Indians killed, 2.

May 14 .... Boulder Creek, Calif. Detachment of Co. B, 4th U. S.
Infty. Indians killed, 14. Indians wounded, 20.

May 29 .... Chaparito, N. M. Detachment of Co. E, Mounted Riflemen. Capt. Thomas Duncan in command. Indians killed,
1. Indians captured, 3. Fight with Comanche Indians.

June 3 .... Redwood Creek, Calif. Co. B, 4th U. S. Infty. 1st Lieut.
J. B. Collins in command. Soldiers wounded, 1. Indians
killed, 8.

June 18 .... Penasco River, N. M. Detachment of Co. C, Mounted
Riflemen, 1st Lieut. G. W. Howland in command.

NOTE: The designation of the **1st U. S. Dragoons** was changed to the
First Regiment of Cavalry on August 3, 1861.

August 5 .... Goose Lake, Calif. Detachment of Tr. F, 1st U. S. Cav.
Lieut. Fielner and 2nd Lieut. J. H. Kellogg in command. In-
dians killed, 1. Indians wounded, 3. Fight with Sheepeater
Apache Indians.

—23—

1862

February 21 .... Valverdo, New Mexico Territory. Trs. D and G, 1st U. S. Cav.

March 1 .... Between Fts. Craig and Union, N. M. Tr. G, 1st U. S. Cavalry. Lieut. W. T. Pennock in command. Soldiers killed, 2. Soldiers wounded, 1.

March 3 .... Comanche Canyon, N. M. Tr. C, and Detachment of Tr. K, 3rd U. S. Cav. Acting 2nd Lieut. R. Wall in command. Acting 2nd Lieut. Wall wounded. Soldiers killed, 1. Soldiers wounded, 2.

March 17 .... Near Ft. Craig, N. M. Tr. D, 1st U. S. Cav.

March 21 .... Pacha Creek, N. M. Tr. G, 1st U. S. Cav.

June 18 .... Canyon Ladrone, N. M. Detachment of Tr. C, 3rd U. S. Cav., 2nd Lieut. Russell in command. Soldiers wounded, 1. Indians killed, 4.

1865

January 1 .... Sycamore Springs, Ariz. Detachment of Co. F, 5th U. S. Infty. Capt. Simon Snyder in command. Indians killed, 4. Fight with the Apache Indians.

January 24 .... Little Cienega, Ariz. Detachment of Co. F, 5th U. S. Infty. Capt. Simon Snyder in command. Soldiers wounded, 2. Indians killed, 20. Fight was with the Apache Indians.

March 24 .... Point of Rocks, 6 miles from Ft. Whipple, Ariz. Detachment of Co. F, 5th U. S. Infty. Capt. Simon Snyder in command. Soldiers wounded, 1. Fight was with the Apache Indians.

December 11 .... Near Peoples' Ranch, Ariz. Detachment of Co. F, 5th U. S. Infty. Capt. Simon Snyder in command. Soldiers killed, 1. Soldiers wounded, 1. Indians killed, 5.

1866

January 12 .... Fish Creek, Nevada. Detachments of Troops B and I, 2nd Calif. Cav., Capt. George D. Conrad in command. Soldiers wounded, 5. Indians killed, 34.

January 21 .... Grant Fort near Cottonwood Springs, Arizona. Detachment of 2nd Calif. Infty. Col. F. Wright in command. Indians killed, 13. Indians captured, 6.

February 15 .... Rock Canon, Guano Valley, Nevada. Detachments of Troops D and F, 2nd Calif. Cav. Major S. P. Smith in command. Soldiers killed, 1. Maj. S. P. Smith wounded. Soldiers wounded, 6. Indians killed, 96. Indians wounded, 15. Indians captured, 19.

February 16 .... Near Jordan Creek, Oregon. Detachments of 2nd Battalion, Co. C, 14th U. S. Infty., and of 1st Oregon Cav. Lieut. Silas Pepoon, 1st Oregon Cav., commanding. Soldiers wounded, 1. Indians killed, 1.

February 23 .... Jordan Creek, Oregon. Detachments of 2nd Battalion, 14th U. S. Infty. and Companies C and D, Oregon Volunteers. Capt. J. H. Walker, 14th U. S. Infty. commanding. Soldiers killed, 1. Soldiers wounded, 1. Indians killed 18. Indians wounded, 2.

March 6—9 .... Palos Blancos and Fort McDowell, Arizona. Detachments of the 1st Arizona Infty. Lieut. Thos. Ewing in command. Indians killed, 20. Indians wounded, 2.

March 20—25 .... Head Waters of Salt River, Arizona. Detachments of 1st Arizona Infty. Lieut. P. Cervantes in command. Indians killed, 22. Indians wounded, 7. Indians captured, 2.

March 22 .... Round Valley, or Cottonwood Springs, Arizona. Detachments of 1st Battalion, 14th U. S. Infty. Capt. J. F. Millar in command. Capt. J. F. Millar and Asst. Surgeon Benj. Tappan, killed. Soldiers killed, 2.

March 28 .... Rita Mangas, New Mexico. Detachments of 1st New Mexico Cav., Troop B. Capt. Nich. Hodt commanding. Indians killed, 1. Indians wounded, 6.

March 31 .... Pimos Village, Arizona. Detachments of Troops B and C, 1st Arizona Infantry and Indian Scouts. Lieut. J. D. Walker in command. Soldiers killed, 1. Soldiers wounded, 2. Indians killed, 25. Indians captured, 16.

April 11 .... Between Fort Lincoln and Fort Whipple, Arizona. Detachments of Troops A and E, 1st Arizona Infantry. Capt. H. S. Washburn in command. Indians killed, 16.

April 22 .... Canon de Chelly, New Mexico. Detachments of 1st Calif. Cav., 1st New Mexico Cav., and 5th Infty. Capt. Edmond Butler, 5th Infty., in command. Indians killed, 26. Indians wounded, 30. Indians captured, 9.

May 27 .... Owyhee River, Idaho (south canon). Detachments of Troops A and C, 2nd Battalion, 14th U. S. Infty. Major L. H. Marshall in command. Soldiers killed, 1. Indians killed, 7. Indians wounded, 12.

July 17 .... Steins Mountain, Oregon. Detachments of Troop C, 14th U. S. Infty. Capt. J. H. Walker in command. Soldiers wounded, 1. Indians killed, 3. Indians wounded, 5.

July 17 .... Reno Creek, Dakota. Detachments of Troops D, E, and F, 2nd Battalion, 18th U. S. Infty. Capt. Henry Haymond in command. Soldiers killed, 1. Soldiers wounded, 4.

July 18 .... Malheur River on Snake Creek, Oregon. Detachment of Troop I, 1st U. S. Cav., with Lieut. R. F. Bernard in command. Soldiers killed, 1. Indians killed, 11.

July 18 .... Rattlesnake Creek, Ore. Detachment of 20 men of Tr. I, 1st U. S. Cav. Sergt. Thomas W. Connor in command. Indians killed, 13. Many Indians wounded. Two horses and two mules captured. Fight was with Shoshone Indians.

July 21 .... Crazy Woman's Fork, Dakota. Detachments of Troop G, 2nd Battalion, 18th Infty., with Capt. T. B. Burrowes. Lieut. N. H. Daniels killed. Soldiers killed, 1.

July 29 .... Owen's Lake, Calif. Detachments of Troop D, 1st Cav. Corporal F. R. Neale in command. Soldiers wounded, 1. Indians killed, 2. Indians captured, 5.

July 29 .... Camp Cady, Calif. Detachments of Troop D, 9th Infty. Lieut. J. R. Hardenbergh commanding. Soldiers killed, 3. Soldiers wounded, 1.

July 31 .... Fort Rice, Dakota. Detachments of 13th Infty. Lieut. J. M. Marshall commanding. Soldiers killed, 1.

August 13 .... Grape Vine Spring, Skull Valley, Ariz. Troop B, 1st Battalion, 14th Infty.; and Co. F, 1st Arizona Infty. Lieut.

O. Hutton, 1st Ariz. Infty., commanding. Soldiers killed, 1. Indians killed, 33. Indians wounded, 40.

August 17 .... Salt River, Arizona. Troop B, 1st Battalion, 14th Infty.; and Troop F, 1st Arizona Infty. Lieut. O. Hutton, 1st Ariz. Infty., commanding. Indians killed, 1. Indians captured, 1.

August 21 .... Paradise Valley, Ore. Tr. M, 1st U. S. Cav. Engagement with Owyhee Indians. Capt. J. C. Hunt in command. Indians killed, 5. Indians routed.

August 24 .... San Francisco Mountains, Arizona. Co. F, 1st Arizona Infty., with Lieut. O. Hutton commanding. Indians wounded, 1. Indians captured, 2.

August 26 .... Owyhee River, Idaho. Troop B, 1st Oregon Cav., and Troop M, 1st U. S. Cav. with Capt. J. C. Hunt, 1st Cav., commanding. Indians killed, 7.

Sept. 10—16 .... Fort Phil Kearny, Dakota. Companies A, C, E, and H, 2nd Battalion, 18th U. S. Infty. Capt. W. J. Fetterman in command. Soldiers killed, 2. Soldiers wounded, 2.

September 11 .... Camp Watson, Oregon. Troop I, 1st U. S. Cav. Capt. E. M. Baker in command. Indians killed, 1. Indians captured, 1.

September 20 .... Fort C. F. Smith, Mont. Companies D, and G, 2nd Battalion, 18th U. S. Infty. Capt. N. C. Kinney in command. Soldiers killed, 2.

September 21 .... Tongue River, Dakota. Companies D and G, 2nd Battalion, 18th U. S. Infty. Capt. N. C. Kinney in command. Soldiers wounded, 2.

September 28 .... Dunder and Blitzen Creek, Idaho. Detachments of Troop M, 1st Cav. Capt. J. C. Hunt in command. Soldiers wounded, 1.

September 28 .... La Bonte Creek, Mont. Troop E, 2nd Cav. Capt. C. E. Norris commanding. Soldiers wounded, 1.

September 29 .... Fort Phil Kearny, Dakota. Companies A, C. E. and H, 18th Infty. Capt. W. J. Fetterman in command. Soldiers killed, 1.

October 3 .... Cedar Valley, Arizona. Tr. E, and Detachment of Tr. C, 1st Cav.; Companies B, D, F, 1st Battalion, 14th Infty. Capt. G. B. Sanford, 1st Cav., in command. Indians killed, 15. Indians captured, 10.

October 3 .... Trinidad, Colo. Troop G, 3rd Cav., and citizens. Major A. J. Alexander, 8th Cav., in command. Soldiers killed, 1. Soldiers wounded, 3. Indians killed, 13.

October 3 .... Long Valley, Nev. Troop A, 1st Cav. Lieut. J. F. Small in command. Indians killed, 8.

October 5 .... Fort Klamath, Ore. Scout to Sprague River. Company I, 1st Oregon Infty. Lieut. H. B. Oatman in command. Indians killed, 4.

October 14 .... Harney Lake Valley, Oregon. Troop I, 1st Cav. Capt. E. M. Baker in command. Soldiers wounded, 1. Indians killed, 3. Indians wounded, 8.

October 15 .... Fort Klamath, Oregon. Co. I, 1st Oregon Infty. Lieut. H. B. Oatman in command. Soldiers wounded, 2. Indians killed, 14. Indians wounded, 20.

October 23 .... North Fork of Platte near Fort Sedgwick, Colo. Troop M, 2nd Cav. Lieut. G. A. Armes in command. Soldiers wounded, 2. Indians killed, 4. Indians wounded, 7.

October 26 .... Lake Albert, Oregon. Detachments of Troop A, 1st Cav. and 1st Oregon Infty. and 5 Klamath Scouts. Lieut. J. F. Small, 1st Cav., in command. Soldiers wounded, 2. Indians killed, 14. Indians captured, 7. Fight with Snake Indians.

October 30 .... Malheur Country, Oregon. Co. E, 23rd Infty. Capt. R. F. O'Beirne in command. Indians killed, 2. Indians wounded, 3. Indians captured, 8.

November 1 .... Trout Creek Canon, Oregon. Company C, 23rd Infty. Capt. J. H. Walker in command. Indians killed, 4 Indians wounded, 3.

November 17 .... Sierra Ancha, Ariz. Troop E, 1st U. S. Cav. Capt. G. B. Sanford commanding. Indians killed, 6. Indians captured, 5.

November 18 .... John Day's River, Oregon. Detachment of 10 men, Troop I, 1st Cav. Lieut. John Barry commanding. Indians killed, 3. Indians wounded, 1.

December 3 .... Camp Watson, Oregon. Detachments of Troop I, 1st Cav. Sergeant T. W. Connor in command. Indians killed, 14. Indians captured, 5.

December 5 .... Surprise Valley, Calif. Detachment of Troop A, 1st Cav. Sergeant J. T. Buckley in command.

December 6 .... Goose Creek, Dakota. Troop C, 2nd Cav., and detachments of Companies A, C, E, and H, 18th Infty. Lieut. H. S. Bingham, 2nd Cav., in command. Lieut. H. S. Bingham killed. Soldiers killed, 1. Soldiers wounded, 2.

December 9—15 .... Near Camp Wallen, Ariz. Detachment of Co. G. 1st U. S. Cav. Skirmish with Apache Indians.

December 11 .... Grief Hill, Ariz. Detachment of Co. C, 1st Battalion, 14th Infty. Capt. G. M. Downey in command. Soldiers killed, 1.

December 14 .... Pinal Mountains, near Camp Wallen, Ariz. Detachment of Co. G, 1st U. S. Cav., Detachment Co. E, 32nd U. S. Infty., Co. E, 14th U. S. Infty. Lieut. W. H. Winters, 1st Cav., in command. Indians killed, 3.

December 21 .... Ft. Phil Kearny, Dak. Co. C, 2nd U. S. Cav.; Co. A, Detachment of Co. C, 18th U. S. Infty.; Cos. A, C, E, H, 27th U. S. Infty. Capt. W. J. Fetterman, 27th U. S. Infty, in command. Capts. W. J. Fetterman, F. H. Brown, and Lieut. G. H. Grummond killed. 49 soldiers of the 18th Infty. and 27 soldiers of Co. C, 2nd Cav., were killed.

December 24 .... Mud Creek, near Ft. Clark, Texas. Detachment of Co. C, 4th U. S. Cav. Capt. J. A. Wilcox in command. Indians wounded, 2.

December 24-25 .... Ft. Buford, Dak. Co. C, 31st U. S. Infty. Capt. W. G. Rankin in command. Indians killed, 3.

December 26 .... Owyhee Creek, Idaho. Co. F, 1st U. S. Cav. Lieut. Col. George Crook, 23rd U. S. Inftry., in command. Soldiers killed, 1. Soldiers wounded, 1. Indians killed, 30. Indians captured, 7.

1867

January 1 .... Ft. Stanton, N. M. Detachment of Tr. H, 3rd U. S. Cav. Sergt. W. Brewster in command. Soldiers wounded, 1. Indians killed, 5.

January 6 .... Crooked River, Oregon. Indian Scouts under Interpreters Darragh and McKay. Soldiers wounded, 1. Indians killed, 26. Indians captured, 8.

January 8 .... Owyhee River, Idaho. Detachment of Tr. M, 1st U. S. Cav., and Indian Scouts. Lieut. Moses Harris in command. 5 Indians killed and wounded.

January 9 .... Malheur River, Ore. Tr. F, 1st U. S. Cav. Lieut. Col. Geo. Crook, 23rd U. S. Infty., in command. Indians captured, 30.

January 18 .... Eden Valley, Nevada. Tr. A, 8th U. S. Cav. Lieut. John Lafferty commanding. Soldiers wounded, 1. Indians killed, 2.

January 19 .... Nueces River, Texas. Detachment of Tr. C, 4th U. S. Cav. Sergt. John Griffin in command. Indians killed, 2.

January 29 .... Owyhee River, or Stein's Mountain, Ore. Tr. M 1st U. S. Cav. Lieut. Col. Geo. Crook, 23rd U. S. Infty., commanding. Citizens killed, 1. Soldiers wounded, 3. Citizens wounded, 1. Indians killed, 60. Indians captured, 27.

January 29 .... Near Camp McDowell, Ariz. Tr. E, 1st U. S. Cav. Capt. G. B. Sanford in command. Indians captured, 1.

February 7 .... Vicksburg Mines, Nev. Tr. B, 1st U. S. Cav. Lieut. G. F. Foote, 9th U. S. Infty., in command. Soldiers wounded, 1.

February 15 .... Black Slate Mountains, Nev. Tr. A, 8th U. S. Cav. Lieut. John Lafferty in command. Indians killed, 6.

February 16 .... Surprise Valley, Calif. Tr. A, 1st U. S. Cav.; Co. C, 9th U. S. Infty. Capt. S. Munson, 9th U. S. Infty., in command. Indians captured, 2. Indians killed, 5.

February 16 .... Warm Springs, Idaho. Tr. M, 1st U. S. Cav. Lieut. Col. Geo. Crook, 23rd U. S. Infty., in command. Indians killed, 2. Indians captured, 5.

February 22—28 Between .... Near Pueblo Mountains, Ore. Tr. H, 1st U. S. Cav. Capt. E. Myers in command. Indians killed, 2. Indian Women and Children captured.

February 23 .... Meadow Valley, Ariz. Tr. E, 1st U. S. Cav. Capt. G. B. Sanford in command. Indians wounded, 1. Soldiers wounded, 1.

February 27 .... Ft. Reno, Dak. Detachments of Cos. B, and I, 27th U. S. Infty. Soldiers killed, 3. Attack on a hunting party from the Fort.

March 2 .... Date Creek, Ariz. Attack on a wagon train.

March 11 ....Arab Canyon, Coso Mountains, Calif. Detachment of Tr. D, 1st U. S. Cav. 1st Sergeant F. R. Neale in command. Indians killed, 12. Chief Babbi killed.

March 12 .... Pecos River, Texas. Detachment of Tr. C, 4th U. S. Cav. Capt. J. A. Wilcox in command. Soldiers killed, 1. Citizens killed, 1. Soldiers wounded, 2. Indians killed, 25.

March 28 .... Murderer's Creek, Ore. Detachment of Tr. F, 8th U. S. Cav. Lieut. C. B. Western, 14th U. S. Infty., in command.

April 3 .... Tonto Valley, Ariz. Capt. Guido Ilges, 14th U. S. Infty., in command. Indians killed, 3. Indians captured, 1.

April 10 .... Black Mountains, Ariz. Detachments of Trs. B and I, 8th U. S. Cav. Capt. J. M. Williams in command. Indians killed, 3.

April 15 .... Ft. Lyon, Colo. Detachment of Tr. C, 7th U. S. Cav. Lieut. Matthew Berry in command. Soldiers wounded, 1.

April 16 .... Black Mountains, Ariz. Trs. B and I, 8th U. S. Cav. Capt. J. M. Williams in command. Indians killed, 20.

April 18 .... Rio Verde, near Black Mountains, Ariz. Trs. B and I, 8th U. S. Cav. Capt. J. M. Williams in command. Soldiers killed, 1. Soldiers wounded, 1. Indians killed, 30.

April 19 .... Cimarron Crossing, Kans. Detachment of Trs. B, and C., 7th U. S. Cav. Lieut. Matthew Berry in command. Soldiers wounded, 1. Indians killed, 6.

April 23 .... Tonto Valley, Ariz. Detachment of Tr. E, 1st U. S. Cav.; Indian Scouts. Bvt. Col. G. B. Sanford in command.

April 24 .... Ft. Mojave, Ariz. Detachment of Trs. B and K, 8th U. S. Cav.; and Co. E., 14th U. S. Infty. Capt. S. B. M. Young, 8th U. S. Cav., in command. Indians killed, 5. Indians wounded, 5.

April 26 .... Ft. Reno, Dak. Co. I, 27th U. S. Infty. Soldiers killed, 1.

April 27 .... Silvie's Creek (near Lake Harney), Ore. Detachment of Tr. F, 8th U. S. Cav. Lieut. C. B. Western, 14th U. S. Infty, in command. Indians killed, 6.

April 27 .... Near Ft. Reno, Dak. Detachments of Cos. D and I, 27th U. S. Infty.

May 1 .... La Prella Creek, Dak. Detachment of Tr. E, 2nd U. S. Cav. Corporal A. Dolfer in command. Soldiers killed, 1.

May 6 .... Mazatzal Mountains, Ariz. Cos. A and B, 32nd U. S. Infty.; Detachment of Cos. A, D, and F, 14th U. S. Infty. Lieut. R. C. De Bois, 14th U. S. Infty., in command. Soldiers wounded, 1. Indians killed, 2.

May 6 .... Four Peaks, Mazatzal Mountains, Ariz. 4 privates of Co. D, 14th U. S. Infty. Attack on a pack train.

May 22 .... Near Camp Watson, Ore. Detachment of Tr. I, 1st U. S. Cav. Sergeant J. H. Jones in command. Indian killed, 1.

May 23 .... Bridger's Ferry, Dak. Detachment of Tr. E, 2nd U. S. Cav. Soldiers killed, 2.

May 23 .... Big Timber, Kans. Stage escort. Soldiers wounded, 1.

May 27 .... Pond Creek Station, Kans. Tr. I, 7th U. S. Cav. Capt. M. W. Keogh in command.

May 30 .... Near Ft. Reno, Dak. Detachment of Co. F, 27th U. S. Infty. Soldiers killed, 1. He was killed while herding.

May 30 .... Near Beale Station, Ariz. Tr. K, 8th U. S. Cav. Lieut. J. D. Stevenson in command. Indians killed, 15.

May 30 .... Beale Station, Ariz. Detachment of Co. E, 14th U. S. Infty. Corporal J. Brown in command. Citizens wounded, 1.

May 31 .... Bluff Ranch, near Ft. Aubrey, Kans. Detachment of Co.

I, 37th U. S. Infty. Soldiers killed, 2. Escort from Ft. Dodge, Kans.

June 1 .... Fairview, Colo. Co. G, 4th U. S. Infty. Capt. P. H. Powell in command. Soldiers killed, 1.

June 5 .... Cimarron Crossing, Kans. Detachment of Co. I, 37th U. S. Infty.

June 8 .... Chalk Bluffs, Kans. Detachment of Tr. F, 7th U. S. Cav. Lieut. H. J. Nowlan in command.

June 11 .... Near Big Timbers, Kans. Detachment of Tr. I, 7th U. S. Cav.; and Co. E, 3rd U. S. Infty. Lieut. J. M. Bell, 7th U. S. Cav., in command Soldiers killed, 1. Mail escort.

June 12 .... Near Ft. Dodge, Kans. Tr. B, 7th U. S. Cav. Lieut. S. A. Brown, 3rd U. S. Infty., in command. Soldiers wounded, 1. Attack on herd near Fort.

June 12 .... Near Ft. Phil. Kearny, Dak. Tr. D, 2nd U. S. Cav. Capt. D. S. Gordon in command. Soldiers killed, 1.

June 14 .... Grinnell Springs, Kans. Detachment of Co. H, 37th U. S. Infty. Soldiers killed, 1.

June 14 .... Yampai Valley, north of Peacock Springs, Ariz. Tr. I, 8th U. S. Cav. Capt. J. M. Williams in command. Indians killed, 20. Indians captured 9.

June 15 .... Big Timbers, Kans. Detachment of Co. E, 3rd U. S. Infty. Soldiers killed, 2. Citizens killed, 1. Soldiers wounded, 1. Citizens wounded, 2. Escort, Ft. Wallace, Kans.

June 16 .... Gallinas Mountains, N. M. Detachment of Tr. H, 3rd U. S. Cav. Sergeant R. Harrington in command. Indians killed, 1. Indians captured, 2.

June 17 .... Cimarron Crossing, Kans. Detachment of Co. I, 37th U. S. Infty.

June 18 .... Near Ft. Phil. Kearny, Dak. Tr. D, 2nd U. S. Cav.

June 19 .... Steins Mountain, Ore. Detachment of Indian Scouts. Chief Scout Archie McIntosh in command. Indians killed, 12. Indians wounded, 1. Indians captured, 2.

June 20 .... Foot of Black Hills, on U. P. R. R., Nebr. Co. C, Pawnee Scouts. Chief Scout Major Frank North in command. Indians killed, 2.

June 21 .... Near Ft. Wallace, Kans. Detachments of Trs. G and I, 7th U. S. Cav. Lieut. J. M. Bell in command. Soldiers killed, 2. Soldiers wounded, 2.

June 21 .... Near Calabases, Ariz. Detachment of Tr. G, 1st U. S. Cav., and Co. E, 32nd U. S. Infty. Lieut. E. J. Harrington in command. Indians killed, 3. Indians wounded, 1. Indians captured, 6.

June 22 .... Goose Creek Station, Colo. Detachment of Co. D, 37th U. S. Infty. Sergeant J. C. McDonald in command. Soldiers wounded, 2.

June 22 .... Near Ft. Wallace, Kans. Detachment of Tr. F, 7th U. S. Cav. Lieut. H. J. Nowlan in command.

June 24 .... North Fork of Republican River, Kans. Trs. A, E, H, K, and M, 7th U. S. Cav. Lieut. Col. G. A. Custer in command. Soldiers wounded, 1.

June 24 .... North Fork of Republican River, Kans. Detachment of

Tr. A, 7th U. S. Cav. Capt. L. M. Hamilton in command. Indians killed, 2.

June 26 .... Wilson's Creek, Kans. Detachment of Co. K, 38th U. S. Infty. Corporal D. Turner in command. Indians killed, 5.

June 26 .... South Fork Republican River, Kans. Detachment of Tr. D, 7th U. S. Cav. Lieut. S. M. Robbins in command. Soldiers wounded, 2. Indians killed, 5.

June 26 .... Near Ft. Wallace, Kans. Tr. G and Detachment of Tr. I, 7th U. S. Cav. Capt. Albert Barnitz in command. Soldiers killed, 6. Soldiers wounded, 6.

June 27 .... Near Ft. Wallace, Kans. Tr. F, 7th U. S. Cav. Lieut. H. J. Nowlan in command.

June 30 .... Near Ft. Phil Kearny, Dak. Co. C, 18th U. S. Infty. Capt. W. P. McCleery in command.

July 1 .... Near Goose Creek, Colo. Detachments of Tr. I, 7th U. S. Cav. and Detachments of Co. E, 3rd U. S. Infty. Soldiers wounded, 1. Escort from post Fort Wallace, Kans.

July 3 .... Bad Lands, Dak. Detachment of Co. A, 4th U. S. Infty.

July 5 .... Dunder and Blitzen Creek, Ore. Trs. F and M, 1st U. S. Cav. and Indian Scouts. Lieut. Col. George Crook, 23rd U. S. Infty., in command. Indians killed, 5. Indians captured, 3.

July 5—11, Between .... Dunder and Blitzen Creek, Ore. Trs. F and M, 1st U. S. Cav., with Capt. David Perry and Lieut. Harris. Gen. Geo. Crook in command. Indians killed, 5. Indians captured, 3.

July 7 .... Beale's Springs, Ariz. Detachment of Tr. K, 8th U. S. Cav. Soldiers killed, 1.

July 7 .... Near Malheur River, Ore. Tr. I, 1st U. S. Cav. Capt. E. M. Baker in command. Indians killed, 2. Indians captured, 14.

July 9 .... Near Truxton Springs, Ariz. Trs. B and I, 8th U. S. Cav. Col. J. I. Gregg in command, Capt. J. M. Williams, 8th Cav., wounded. Soldiers wounded, 1. Indians killed, 3.

July 9 .... Near Ft. Stevenson, Dak. Co. C and Detachments of Cos. D. and F., 10th U. S. Infty.

July 9 .... Near Ft. Sumner, N. M. Detachments of Trs. G. and I., 3rd U. S. Cav. Lieut. Chas. Porter, 5th U. S. Infty. in command. Soldiers killed, 5. Soldiers wounded, 4.

July 11 .... Bluff Ranch, Kans. Detachment of Co. I., 37th U. S. Infty.

July 13 .... South Fork Malheur River, Ore. Detachment of Co. K., 23rd U. S. Infty.; and Snake Indians. Lieut. G. A. Goodale in command. Soldiers killed, 1. Indians killed, 5. Indians captured, 2.

July 15 .... Ft. Aubrey, Kans. Detachment of Co. I., 37th U. S. Infty.

July 17 .... Downer's Station, Kans. Detachments of Trs. H. and K., 7th U. S. Cav.

July 19 .... Malheur Country, Ore. Tr. I., 1st U. S. Cav. Capt. E. M. Baker in command. Indians killed, 2. Indians captured, 8.

July 21 .... Buffalo Springs, Texas. Detachments of Trs. A. and E.,

6th U. S. Cav. Lieut. T. C. Tupper in command. Indians killed, 1.

July 21 .... Cimarron Crossing, Kans. Detachment of Co. I., 37th U. S. Infty.

July 22 .... Beaver Creek, Kans. Detachment of Tr. M., 2nd U. S. Cav. Lieut. L. S. Kidder in command. Lieut. Lyman S. Kidder killed. Soldiers killed, 10. Bearing dispatches.

July 27 .... Between Camps C. F. Smith and Harney, Ore. Trs. F. and M., 1st U. S. Cav.; and Indian Scouts. Lieut. Col. Geo. Crook, 23rd U. S. Infty., in command. 46 Indians killed and wounded.

July 29 .... Near Ft. Hays, Kans. Detachment of Co. G., 38th U. S. Infty.

July 29 .... Willows, Ariz. Detachment of Tr. A, 8th U. S. Cav.

August 1 .... Near Ft. C. F. Smith, Mont. Detachments from Cos. D., C., G., H., and I., 27th U. S. Infty. Lieut. Sigismund Sternberg in command. Lieut. Sternberg killed. Soldiers killed, 1. Citizens killed, 1. Indians killed, 8. Indians wounded, 30.

August 1 .... Willow Creek, Ariz. Detachment of Co. H., 14th U. S. Infty.

August 2 .... Near Ft. Phil Kearny, Dak. Cos. A., C., and F., 27th U. S. Infty. Capt. James Powell in command. Lieut. J. C. Jenness killed. Soldiers killed, 5. Soldiers wounded, 2. Indians killed, 60. Indians wounded, 120.

August 2 .... Saline River, Kans., Tr. F., 10th U. S. Cav. Capt. G. A. Armes in command. Capt. Armes wounded. Soldiers killed, 1.

August 8 .... Ft. Stevenson, Dak. Detachments of Cos. H., and I., 31st U. S. Infty. Capt. A. M. Powell in command. Citizens killed, 1.

August 11-14 .... Owyhee River, Ore. Co. A. and Detachment of Co. E., 23rd U. S. Infty.

August 13 .... O'Connor's Springs, Dak. Co. B. and Detachment of Co. A, 27th U. S. Infty. Capt. H. B. Freeman in command. Soldiers wounded, 3.

August 14 .... Ft. Reno, Dak. Detachment of Co. G., 18th U. S. Infty. Lieut. F. F. Whitehead in command.

August 14 .... Chalk Springs, Dak. Co. E, 27th U. S. Infty. Soldiers killed, 1.

August 15 .... Ft. Aubrey, Kans. Detachment of Co. I., 37th U. S. Infty.

August 16 .... Near Ft. Reno, Dak. Cattle Herders. Citizens killed, 2.

August 17 .... Near Plum Creek, Nebr. Pawnee Scouts. Capt. Jas. Murie, Chief Pawnee Scout, in command. Indians killed, 15. Indians wounded, 2.

August 21—22 .... Prairie Dog Creek, Kans. Tr. F., 10th U. S. Cav. and Detachment of 18th Kansas Infty. Capt. G. A. Armes in command. Soldiers killed, 3. Soldiers wounded, 35. Indians killed, 150.

August 22 .... Mountain Pass, near Ft. Chadbourne, Texas. Detachments of Trs. D., G., and H., 4th U. S. Cav. Sergeant B. Jenkins in command. Soldiers killed, 2. Acting as Escort.

August 22 .... Surprise Valley, Calif. Boise Indian Scouts. Chief Scout Archie McIntosh in command. Indians killed, 2. Indians wounded, 7.

August 23 .... Near North Concho River, Texas. Detachment of Tr. A., 4th U. S. Cav. Soldiers killed, 1.

August 28 .... Camp Goodwin, Ariz. One Herder wounded.

August 30 .... Near Ft. Belknap, Texas. Tr. F., 6th U. S. Cav. Lieut. Gustavus Schreyer in command. Soldiers killed, 2.

September 6 .... Near Silver River, Ore. Tr. A., 1st U. S. Cav. Lieut. J. F. Small in command. Indians killed, 1. Indians captured, 5.

September 8 .... Silver River, Ore. Tr. A., 1st U. S. Cav. Lieut. J. F. Small in command. Soldiers wounded, 2. Indians killed, 23. Indians captured, 14.

September 10 .... Live Oak Creek, Texas. Detachment of Tr. K., 4th U. S. Cav. Lieut. N. J. McCafferty in command.

September 16 .... Near Ft. Inge, Texas. Detachment of Tr. K., 4th U. S. Cav. Lieut. N. J. McCafferty in command.

September 16 .... Saline River, Kans. Detachment of Tr. G., 10th U. S. Cav. Sergeant C. H. Davis in command. Citizens killed, 2. Soldiers wounded, 1.

September 19 .... Walker's Creek, 35 miles west of Ft. Harker, Kans. Detachment of Co. K., 5th U. S. Infty. Lieut. Mason Carter in command. Soldiers killed, 1. Soldiers wounded, 3. Indians killed, 1.

September 20 .... Near Devil's River, Texas. Detachment of Tr. C., 4th U. S. Cav. Lieut. D. A. Irwin in command. Indians killed, 1.

September 22 .... Pawnee Fork Bluff, Kans. Detachment of Co. A., 3rd U. S. Infty.

September 23 .... Arkansas River, 9 miles west of Cimarron Crossing, Kans. Co. K., 5th U. S. Infty. Capt. D. H. Brotherton in command. Lieut. Ephraim Williams wounded. Soldiers killed, 1.

September 24 .... Nine Mile Ridge, Kans. Detachment of Co. I., 37th U. S. Infty. Soldiers wounded, 1. Escort duty.

September 25 .... Bluff Ranch, Kans. Detachment of Co. I., 37th U. S. Infty.

September 26—28 .... Infernal Caverns, near Pitt River, Calif. Tr. H., 1st U. S. Cav.; Co. D., 23rd U. S. Infty.; and Boise Indian Scouts. Lieut. Col. Geo. Crook, 23rd U. S. Infty., in command. Lieut. J. Madigan, 1st Cav., killed. Soldiers killed, 6. Citizens killed, 1. Soldiers wounded, 11. Indians killed, 20. Indians wounded, 12. Indians captured, 2.

September 29 .... Pretty Encampment, near Ft. Garland, Colo. Detachment of Co. G., 37th U. S. Infty. Soldiers killed, 2.

October 1 .... Howard's Well, Texas. Detachment of Tr. D., 9th U. S. Cav. Corporal S. Wright in command. Soldiers killed, 2. Mail escort.

October 4 .... Near Camp Logan, Ore. Detachment of Tr. E, 8th U. S. Cav. Lieut. James Pike, 1st U. S. Cav., in command.

October 6 .... Trout Creek, Ariz. Tr. L., 8th U. S. Cav. Lieut. A. B. Wells in command. Indians killed, 7.

October 10 .... Near Camp Lincoln, Ariz. Detachments of Cos. C. and G., 14th U. S. Infty. Capt. David Krause in command. Indians killed, 1.

October 10 .... Ft. Stevenson, Dak. Detachment of Co. H., 31st U. S. Infty. Soldiers wounded, 1.

October 17 .... Deep Creek, Texas. Detachments of Trs. F., I., K., and L., 6th U. S. Cav. Sergeant W. A. F. Ahrberg in command. Indians killed, 3. Indians captured, 1.

October 18 .... Sierra Diablo, N. M. Trs. D. and K., 3rd U. S. Cav. Capt. F. H. Wilson in command. Soldiers killed, 1. Soldiers wounded, 6. 25 or 30 Indians killed or wounded.

October 20 .... Crazy Woman's Fork, Dak. Indians killed, 1.

October 22—26, Between .... Owyhee River, Ore. Detachment of Tr. H, 1st U. S. Cav. Troop en route to Ft. Boise, Idaho.

October 25 .... Truxton Springs, Ariz. Tr. L., 8th U. S. Cav. Lieut. A. B. Wells in command. Indians killed, 1.

October 26 .... Shell Creek, Dak. Tr. D., 2nd U. S. Cav. Capt. D. S. Gordon in command. On a scout.

October 26 .... Near Camp Winfield Scott, Nev. Tr. L., 1st U. S. Cav.; Tr. A, 8th U. S. Cav. Capt. J. P. Baker, 1st U. S. Cav., in command. Indians killed, 3. Indians captured, 4.

November 3 .... Willow Grove, Ariz. Detachment of Tr. E., 1st U. S. Cav.; Detachment of Tr. L., 8th U. S. Cav. Lieut. Patrick Hasson, 14th U. S. Infty., in command. Indians killed, 32.

November 4 .... Goose Creek, Dak. Detachments of Trs. D., E., G., H., and I., 27th U. S. Infty. Lieut. E. R. P. Shurly in command. Lieut. Shurly wounded Soldiers killed, 1. Soldiers wounded, 3.

November 5 .... Near Camp Bowie, Ariz. Lieut. J. C. Carroll, 32nd U. S. Infty., and 1 citizen. Lieut. Carroll killed. Citizens wounded, 1.

November 6 .... Near Ft. Buford, Dak. Detachment of Co. C., 31st U. S. Infty.

November 7 .... Toll Gate, Ariz. Tr. L., 8th U. S. Cav. Lieut. A. B. Wells in command. Indians killed, 3.

November 8 .... Near Willows, Ariz. Detachment of Tr. E., 1st U. S. Cav., and Detachment of Tr. L., 8th U. S. Cav. Lieut. Patrick Hasson, 14th U. S. Infty., in command. Lieut. Hasson wounded. Soldiers wounded, 5. Indians killed, 19. Indians captured, 17.

November 11 .... Camp Lincoln, Ariz. Detachment of Co. C., 14th U. S. Infty. Soldiers wounded, 3.

November 13 .... Aqua Frio Springs, near Camp Lincoln, Ariz. Detachment of Co. C., 14th U. S. Infty. Lieut. O. I. Converse in command. Lieut. Converse was wounded. Soldiers wounded, 2.

November 13 .... Crazy Woman's Fork of Powder River, Mont. A Detachment of recruits of the 27th U. S. Infty.

November 14-15 .... Near Tonto Creek, Ariz. Detachment of Indian Scouts. Indians killed, 4. Indians captured, 9.

November 17 .... Near Ft. Sumner, N. M. Co. F., 37th U. S. Infty. Soldiers killed, 1.

November 17 .... Willow Grove, Ariz. Detachment of Tr. K., 8th
U. S. Cav.
November 20 .... Near Ft. Seldon, N. M. Tr. K., 3rd U. S. Cav.
Lieut. Oscar Elting in command. Indians killed, 2.
November 22 .... De Schmidt Lake, Dak. Tr. D., 2nd U. S. Cav. Capt.
D. S. Gordon in command. Indians killed, 1. Indians wound-
ed, 3.
November 29 .... Shell Creek, Dak. Tr. D., 2nd U. S. Cav. Capt.
D. S. Gordon in command. Indians killed, 4.
December 2 .... Crazy Woman's Creek, Dak. Detachment of Co.
C., 18th U. S. Infty. Sergeant G. Gillaspy in command.
Soldiers killed, 1. Citizens wounded, 4. Soldiers wounded,
3.
December 2 .... Near Willows, Ariz. Detachment of Tr. E., 1st U.
S. Cav.; Detachment of Co. L., 8th U. S. Cav.
December 5 .... Eagle Springs, Tex. Detachment of Tr. F., 9th U. S.
Cav. Soldiers killed, 1.
December 12 .... Owyhee River, Ore. Indian Scouts. Interpreter
D. C. Pickett in command. Indians killed, 7.
December 14 .... Near Ft. Phil Kearny, Dak. Indians attacked some
wood-cutters. Citizens wounded, 2.
December 19 .... San Pedro River, near Camp Wallen, Ariz. De-
tachment of Tr. G., 1st U. S. Cav. Lieut. W. H. Winters in
command. Indians killed, 1.
December 26 .... Near Ft. Lancaster, Texas. Detachment of Co. K.,
9th U. S. Cav. Capt. W. T. Frohock in command. Soldiers
killed, 3. Indians killed, 20. Indians wounded, 11.

1868
January .... Ft. Quitman, Texas. Detachment of Tr. E, 9th U. S.
Cav.
January 4 .... Near Owyhee River, Ore. Detachment of Tr. M, 1st
U. S. Cav.; Indian scouts. Interpreter D. C. Pickett in com-
mand. Indians killed, 1. Indians captured, 15.
January 14 .... Difficult Canyon, Ariz. Tr. K, 8th U. S. Cav. Capt.
S. B. M. Young in command. Soldiers wounded, 2. Indians
killed, 16. Indians wounded, 6.
January 14 .... Beale Springs, Ariz. Tr. K, 8th U. S. Cav. Lieut.
J. D. Stevenson in command. Lieut. Stevenson wounded. In-
dians killed, 5.
January 16 .... Near Kenny's ranch, Malheur River, Ore. Tr. D, 8th
U. S. Cav. Capt. Abraham Bassford in command. (Heit-
man gives the date of this battle as February 16.)
February 14 .... Steins Mountains, Ore. Tr. H, 1st U. S. Cav.; 30
Mounted Infantrymen, and 14 Indian Scouts. Lieut. W. R.
Parnell, 1st U. S. Cav., in command. 14 Indians killed and
captured.
March 6 .... Paint Creek, Texas. Trs. F, I, and K, of 6th U. S. Cav.
Capt. A. R. Chaffee in command. Soldiers wounded, 2. In-
dians killed, 7.
March 10 .... Head of Colorado River, Texas. Detachment of Tr.
D, 4th U. S. Cav. Sergeant C. Gale in command. Indians
killed, 1.

March 11 .... Near Tularosa, N. M. Citizens killed, 13. Apache Indians raided settlements. Pursued by Tr. H, 3rd Cav. under Lieut. P. D. Vroom.

March 14 .... Dunder and Blitzen Creek, Ore. Tr. H, 1st U. S. Cav.; Tr. C, 8th U. S. Cav.; Co. D, 23rd U. S. Infty. Lieut. Col. George Crook, 23rd U. S. Infty., in command. Lieut. W. R. Parnell, 1st U. S. Cav., wounded. Soldiers wounded, 2. Indians killed, 12. Indians captured, 2.

March 18 .... Near Saw Mill, Ft. Fetterman, Dak. Detachment of Co. K, 18th U. S. Infty. Soldiers killed, 1.

March 20 .... Horseshoe and Twin Springs Ranches, Dak. Citizens killed, 3.

March 21 .... Near Camp Willow Grove, Ariz. Detachment of Co. E. 14th U. S. Infty. Corporal D. Troy in command. Soldiers killed, 2. Escort duty.

March 21 .... Dunder and Blitzen Creek, Ore. Detachment of Tr. H, 1st U. S. Cav.

March 25 .... Cottonwood Springs, Ariz. Detachment of Co. B, 14th U. S. Infty. Capt. Guido Ilges in command. Soldiers wounded, 1. Indians killed, 1. Indians wounded, 2.

March 25 .... Bluff Creek, Kans. Settlers attacked by Indians. No details reported.

March 26 .... Owyhee River, Ore. Detachment of Tr. D, 8th U. S. Cav. Sergeant John New in command. Indians killed, 1.

April 1 .... Pinal Mountains, Ariz. Tr. G, 1st U. S. Cav. Lieut. W. H. Winters in command.

April 3 .... Rock Creek, Wyo. Attack on wood party. Indians killed, 1.

April 5 .... Malheur River, Ore. Tr. F, 1st U. S. Cav.; Tr. C, 8th U. S. Cav.; Detachment of Co. K, 23rd U. S. Infty.; and Indian Scouts. Capt. David Perry, 1st Cav., in command. Indians killed, 32. Indians captured, 2.

April 15 .... Ft. C. F. Smith, Mont. Detachment of Co. D, 27th U. S. Infty.

April 17 .... Camp Three Forks, Owyhee, Idaho. Co. E, 23rd U. S. Infty. Capt. G. K. Brady in command. Indians killed, 5. Indians captured, 3.

April 17 .... Nesmith's Mills, near Tulerosa, N. M. Detachment of Tr. H, 3rd U. S. Cav., and citizens. Sergeant E. Glass in command. Soldiers wounded, 1. Citizens wounded, 5. Indians killed, 10. Indians wounded, 25.

April 21 .... Near Camp Grant, Ariz. Tr. I, 8th U. S. Cav. Capt. E. G. Fechet in command. Indians killed, 2.

April 21 .... Upper Yellowstone River, Mont. Citizens killed, 1.

April 22 .... Near Ft. McPherson, Nebr. Attack on herd. Citizens killed, 6.

April 22—24 .... Near Ft. McPherson, Nebr. Detachments of Trs. B and C, 2nd U. S. Cav.

April 23 .... Near Camp Harney, Ore. Detachment of Scouts. Chief Guide Archie McIntosh in command. Indians killed, 1.

April 23 .... Near Ft. Ellis, Mont. Citizens killed, 1.

April 29 .... Camp Winfield Scott, Paradise Valley, Nev. Tr. A, 8th

U. S. Cav. Lieut. Pendleton Hunter in command. Lieut. Hunter wounded. Soldiers wounded, 2.

April 29 .... South of Otseos Lodge, Warner Mountains, Ore. Detachment of Co. D, 23rd U. S. Infty. Lieut. A. H. Nickerson in command. Soldiers wounded, 2.

May 1 .... Near Camp Crittenden, Ariz. Tr. C., 1st U. S. Cav. Capt. Harrison Moulton in command. Soldiers wounded, 1.

May 1 ....San Pedro River, Ariz. Tr. E, 1st U. S. Cav. Lieut. C. C. C. Carr in command. Indians killed, 3.

May 1 .... Gila River, near Camp Grant, Ariz. Tr. I, 8th U. S. Cav. Capt. E. G. Fechet in command. Indians killed, 6. Indians wounded, 4.

May 1 .... Hoag's Bluff, Warner Valley, Ore. Detachment of Tr. G, 8th U. S. Cav.; Co. C, 9th U. S. Infty. Capt. S. Munson, 9th U. S. Infty., in command. Citizens killed, 1. Lieut. Hayden DeLany, 9th U. S. Infty., wounded. Soldiers wounded, 1.

May 13 .... Near Ft. Buford, Dak. Citizens killed, 2.

May 15 .... Between Fts. Stevenson and Totten, Dak. Citizens killed, 2.

May 17 .... Attack on Camp Cooke, Mont. Cos. B and H, 13th U. S. Infty.

May 18 .... Rio Salinas, Ariz. Trs. B and L, 8th U. S. Cav. Lieut. Robert Carrick in command. Indians killed, 6.

May 19 .... Mouth of Musselshell River, Dak. Co. E and Detachments of Cos. B and H, 13th U. S. Infty. Capt. Robert Nugent in command. Indians wounded, 10.

May 24 .... Mouth of Musselshell River, Mont. Detachments of Cos. B, F, and H, 13th U. S. Infty. Lieut. A. N. Canfield in command. Soldiers killed, 2.

May 24 .... Near Yellowstone River, Mont. Detachment of Co. F, 13th U. S. Infty., and citizens. Sergeant James Keating in command.

May 29 .... Camp Lyon, near Owyhee River, Idaho. Detachment of Tr. M, 1st U. S. Cav., and Indian Scouts. Sergeant H. Miller in command. Indians killed, 34.

May 30 .... Tonto Basin, San Carlos trail, Ariz. Trs. B and L, 8th U. S. Cav. Lieut. Col. T. C. Devin in command. Citizens killed, 1. Soldiers wounded, 1.

May 31 .... Castle Rock, near North Fork Malheur River, Ore. Detachment of Tr. F, 1st U. S. Cav. Lieut. A. H. Stanton in command. Soldiers wounded, 1. Indians captured, 5. Skirmish with Pi-Ute Indians.

June 6 .... Near Ft. Sumner, N. M. Detachments of Trs. G and I, 3rd U. S. Cav. Capt. D. Monahan in command. Citizens killed, 4. Indians killed, 3. Indians wounded, 11. Fight was with Navajo Indians.

June 8—15 .... Apache Springs, N. M. Detachments of Trs. G and I, 3rd U. S. Cav. Lieut. Deane Monahan in command. Indians wounded, 11.

June 9 .... Snake Canyon, Idaho. Detachment of Co. H, 23rd U. S. Infty., and Indian Scouts. Corporal J. Moan in command. Indians killed, 3.

June 13 .... Twenty-five Yard Creek, Mont. Detachment of Co. F, 13th U. S. Infty. Capt. J. L. Horr in command.

June 16 .... Toddy Mountains, Ariz. Detachment of Tr. E, 1st U. S. Cav. Sergeant J. Lemon in command. Soldiers killed, 4. Indians killed, 1. On mail escort.

June 24 .... Near Battle Creek, Idaho. Co. A, 23rd U. S. Infty. Capt. J. J. Coppinger in command. Indians killed, 3. Indians captured, 3.

June 25 .... Near Ft. Hays, Kans. A detachment of troops attacked and pursued a band of hostile Indians, but no casualties occurred.

July 4 .... Near Ft. Phil Kearny, Dak. Co. I, 27th U. S. Infty.

July 5 .... Near Ft. Phil Kearny, Dak. Detachment of Co. A, 27th U. S. Infty.

July 8 .... Between Verde and Salt rivers, Ariz. Detachment of Tr. E, 1st U. S. Cav.; and Tr. I, 8th U. S. Cav. Lieut. C. C. C. Carr, 1st U. S. Cav., in command. Indians killed, 1.

July 11 .... Near Niobrara River. Attack on herd. Citizens killed, 1. Soldiers wounded, 1.

July 17 .... Stein's Mountain, Ore. Co. C, 23rd U. S. Infty., and Indian scouts.

July 18 .... Near Ft. Phil. Kearny, Dak. Co. I, 27th U. S. Infty.

July 19 .... Near Ft. Reno, Nev. Detachment of Tr. A, 2nd U. S. Cav., and Cos. B and F, 27th U. S. Infty. Lieut. E. R. P. Shurly, 27th U. S. Infty., in command. Soldiers killed, 1. Soldiers wounded, 1.

July 22 .... Near Camp Crittenden, Ariz. Detachment of Tr. K, 1st U. S. Cav.

July 25 .... Scout on Big Salmon River, Idaho. Detachment of Co. H, 23rd U. S. Infty., and Indian Scouts. Capt. J. B. Sinclair in command. Indians captured, 41.

July 26 .... Juniper Canyon, Idaho. Detachment of Co. E, 23rd U. S. Infty. 2nd Lieut. G. McM. Taylor in command. Indians killed, 5. Indians captured, 4.

July 28 .... Near Sully's Old Camp, Dak. Detachments of Cos. B, C, and E, 31st U. S. Infty. Lieut. C. C. Cusick in command.

July 30 .... Tonto Valley, near Camp Reno, Ariz. Detachment of Co. A, 32nd U. S. Infty. Lieut. W. F. Denney in command. Soldiers wounded, 1.

July 30 .... On Republican River, Nebr. (on line of U. P. R. R.) Detachment of Indian scouts.

August 2 .... Cimarron River, Kans. Tr. K, 7th U. S. Cav. Capt. R. M. West in command.

August 6 .... Ft. Quitman, Texas. Tr. H. 9th U. S. Cav.

August 8—September 5 .... Juniper Mountains, Idaho. Detachment of Co. A, 23rd U. S. Infty., and Indian Scouts. Sergeant T. Slatter in command. Indians captured, 16.

August 10 .... Saline River, Kans. 225 Cheyennes, Arapahoes and Sioux attacked and plundered a small settlement.

August 10 .... Near the Cimmaron River, Kans. Indians attacked a column of troops under Gen. Alfred Sully, 3rd U. S. Infty. Soldiers killed, 1. Indians killed, 12. Indians wounded, 12.

August 12 .... Saline River, Kans. Detachment of Tr. H, 7th U. S. Cav. Capt. F. W. Benteen in command.

August 12 .... Southern, Kans. Troops under Gen. Alfred Sully, 3rd U. S. Infty., attacked. Soldiers killed, 2. Soldiers wounded, 3. Indians killed, 12. Indians wounded, 15.

August 12 .... Solomon River, Kans. Band of Cheyennes, Arapahoes and Sioux raided the settlement. Citizens killed, 17. Citizens wounded, 4.

August 12 .... Republican River, Kans. Citizens killed, 2.

August 13 .... Walnut Grove, Ariz. Tr. L, 8th U. S. Cav. Lieut. A. B. Wells in command. Indians killed, 3.

August 13 .... Saline River, Kans. Detachment of Tr. H, and M. 7th U. S. Cav. Capt. F. W. Benteen in command. Indians killed, 3. Indians wounded, 10.

August 13 .... Southern Kansas. General Alfred Sully's command again attacked. Soldiers killed, 1. Soldiers wounded, 4. Indians killed, 10. Indians wounded, 12.

August 14 .... Granny Creek, Kans. (On the Republican River) Citizens killed, 1. Citizens wounded, 1. Citizens captured, 1; a woman.

August 14 .... Near Ft. Zarah, Kans. Indians ran off 20 mules but they were recaptured by troops. Citizens wounded, 1. Indians killed, 1. Indians wounded, 5.

August 18 .... Pawnee Fork, Kans. Indians attacked a train. Cavalry from Ft. Dodge dispersed them. Citizens wounded, 5. Indians killed, 5. Indians wounded, 10.

August 19 .... Twin Butte Creek, Kans. Party of wood choppers attacked by 30 Indians. Citizens killed, 3.

August 20 .... Ft. Buford, Dak. Cos. B, C, E, and G, 31st U. S. Infty. Capt. C. J. Dickey in command. Soldiers killed, 3. Lieut. C. C. Cusick, wounded. Soldiers wounded, 3.

August 20 .... Comstock's Ranch, Kans. Citizens killed, 2. Citizens wounded, 1.

August 22 .... Santa Maria River, Ariz. Tr. B, 8th U. S. Cav. Lieut. Rufus Somerby in command. Indians killed, 2. Indians captured, 1.

August 22 .... Sheridan, Kans. Indians attacked and ran off stock.

August 23 .... Between Pond Creek, Kans., and Lake Station, Colo. Denver Stage Coach attacked by Indians.

August 23 .... Stage to Cheyenne Wells forced to return, was chased ed 4 miles by 30 Indians.

August 23 .... Bent's Fort on the Arkansas River. Attacked by Indians and stock run off.

August 23 .... Near Fort Totten, Dak. Detachments of Cos. A, B, and K, 31st U. S. Infty. Soldiers killed, 3.

August 24 .... Near Bent's Fort, on the Arkansas River. Three stage coaches and one wagon train attacked.

August 25 .... Near Ft. Dodge, Kans. Indians killed herder. Acting Governor Hall of Colorado reported a band of two hundred Indians devastating Southern Colorado.

August 27 .... Between Ft. Lyon, Colo., and Ft. Sheridan, Kans. Capt. H. C. Bankhead, 5th U. S. Infty., reported 13 Indians killed a citizen named Woodworth.

August 27 .... Big Springs, Kans. Band of 250 Indians attacked train of Capt. Edmond Butler, 5th U. S. Infty.

August 27 .... Hatchet Mountains, N. M. Co. F, 38th U. S. Infty. Capt. Alex. Moore in command. Indians killed, 3.

August 28 .... Near Kiowa Station, Kans. Citizens killed, 3. 50 head of stock driven off.

August 28 .... Near Platte River, Nebr. Co. A, Pawnee Scouts. Capt. C. E. Morse in command.

August 29 .... Near Ft. Lyon, Kans. Capt. W. H. Penrose, 3rd U. S. Infty., reported a train of 13 wagons attacked by Indians. The men escaped to Ft. Lyon.

August 30 .... Republican River, Nebr. Cos. A and B, Pawnee Scouts.

August 31 .... Kiowa Creek, Kans. Lieut. T. A. Reily, 5th U. S. Infty. reported Indians had run off 200 horses and 40 cattle from stage company's station.

September 1 .... Lake Station, Colo. Citizens killed, 2. 30 head of stock run off.

September 1 .... Reed's Springs, Colo. Citizens killed, 3. Citizens wounded, 3.

September 1 .... Spanish Fort, Texas. Citizens killed, 9. Citizens scalped, 8. 15 horses and mules run off.

September 2 .... Little Coon Creek, Kans. Detachments of Tr. B, 7th U. S. Cav.; Detachment of Cos. A and F, 3rd U. S. Infty. Mail escort. Corporal J. Goodwin in command. Attacked by about 40 Indians. Soldiers wounded, 3. Indians killed, 3. Indians wounded, 1.

September 3 .... Hugo Springs, Colo. Attacked by large body of Indians but repulsed by guards.

September 3 .... Colorado City, Colo. Citizens killed, 4.

September 4 .... Tonto Creek, Ariz. Tr. E, 1st U. S. Cav.; Tr. I, 8th U. S. Cav.; and Indian Scouts. Major A. J. Alexander, 8th U. S. Cav., in command. Indians killed, 1. Indians captured, 1.

September 5 .... Willow Springs Station, Colo. Indians burned the station.

September 6—7 .... Colorado Territory. Citizens killed, 25.

September 8 .... Clark's train on Turkey Creek, Kans. Indians drove off 76 horses and mules.

September 8 .... Cimarron Crossing, Kans. Citizens killed, 17. 45 wagons in two trains, and 65 men, were attacked by Indians. Lieut. D. W. Wallingford, 7th U. S. Cav., and detachment was sent to rescue.

September 8 .... Near Sheridan, Kans. 25 Indians killed 2 citizens.

September 9 .... Between Sheridan and Ft. Wallace, Kans. Indians burned a ranch and killed 6 citizens.

September 9 .... Tonto Plateau, Ariz. Detachment of Tr. B, 8th U. S. Cav. Lieut. Rufus Somerby in command. Indians killed, 2. Indians captured, 4.

September 10 .... Rule Creek, or Purgatory River, Colo. Tr. L, 7th U. S. Cav. Capt. W. H. Penrose, 3rd U. S. Infty., in command. Soldiers killed, 2. Soldiers wounded, 1. Indians killed, 4.

September 10 .... Near Lake Station, Colo. Capt. Edmond Butler, 5th U. S. Infty., Ft. Wallace, reported a stage fired into.

September 10 .... Lower Aqua Fria, Ariz. Tr. B, 8th U. S. Cav. Lieut. Rufus Somerby in command. Indians killed, 4. Indians captured, 3.

September 11 .... Rio Verde, Ariz. Tr. B, 8th U. S. Cav. Lieut. Rufus Somerby in command. Indians killed, 5.

September 11—15 .... Sand Hill, Indian Territory, Trs. A, B, C. D, E, F. G, I, and K, 7th U. S. Cav.; Co. F, 3rd U. S. Infty. Gen. Alfred Sully, 3rd U. S. Infty., in command. Soldiers killed, 3. Soldiers wounded, 5. Indians killed, 22. Indians wounded, 12.

September 12 .... Near Ft. Reynolds, Colo. Gen. W. A. Nichols, Assistant Adjutant-General, in charge of Escort Guard which was attacked by Indians, and driven off.

September 13 .... Dragoon Fork of Verde River, Ariz. Tr. B, 8th U. S. Cav. Lieut. Rufus Somerby in command. Soldiers wounded, 1. Indians killed, 2.

September 14 .... Horse Head Hills, Texas. Detachments of Trs. C, F, and K, 9th U. S. Cav. Lieut. Patrick Cusack in command. Soldiers wounded, 1. Indians killed, 25. Indians wounded, 25.

September 15 .... Big Sandy Creek, Colo. Tr. I, 10th U. S. Cav. Capt. G. W. Graham in command. Soldiers attacked by 100 Indians. Soldiers wounded, 7. Indians killed, 11. Indians wounded, 14.

September 17 .... Ellis Station, Kans. Settlement was burned and one man killed.

September 17 .... Near Ft. Bascom, N. M. Indians killed a herder and ran off 30 mules. Troops from the fort chased Indians 125 miles.

September 17 .... Settlements on the Saline River, Kans. Detachment of 7th U. S. Cav. Soldiers wounded, 3. Indians killed, 3. Indians wounded, 5.

September 17-25 .... Arickaree Fork of Republican River, Kans. Company of 50 scouts. Col. G. A. Forsyth, 9th U. S. Cav., and Lieut. Frederick H. Beecher, 3rd U. S. Infty., in command. Lieut. F. H. Beecher and Surgeon John H. Moore killed. Col. G. A. Forsyth wounded twice. Capt. L. H. Carpenter's company of the 10th U. S. Cav. came to the rescue September 25. Citizens killed, 4. Citizens wounded, 15. Indians killed, 35.

September 19 .... Near Big Timber, Kans. Capt. H. C. Bankhead, 5th U. S. Infty., Ft. Wallace, reported 15 Indians had fired into a ranch.

September 26 .... Near Ft. Rice, Dak. Cos. A, B, I, and H, 22nd U. S. Infty. Soldiers killed, 1.

September 29 .... Sharp's Creek, Kans. Citizens killed, 1. Burned the house, killed the husband, and left wife and child to die.

September 30 .... Big Bend, Kans. Co. D, 3rd U. S. Infty.

October 2 .... Attack on Ft. Zarah, Kans. Attacked by 100 Indians. Co. D, 3rd U. S. Infty.

October 2 .... Between Fts. Larned and Dodge, Kans. Co. E, 3rd U.

S. Infty. Gen. Alfred Sully reported attack on train. Citizens killed, 3. Citizens wounded, 3.

October 3 .... Mimbres Mountains, N. M. Detachment of Tr. E, 3rd U. S. Cav. Sergeant C. Brown in command. Soldiers killed, 1.

October 3 .... Cow Creek, Kans. Detachment of Co. D, 3rd U. S. Infty.

October 4 .... Near Ft. Dodge, Kans. Citizens killed, 2. Citizens wounded, 1.

October 7 .... Purgatory River, Colo. Citizens killed, 1.

October 9 .... Salt River and Cherry Creek, Ariz. Tr. E, 1st U. S. Cav.; Tr. I, 8th U. S. Cav.; Co. F, 14th U. S. Infty.; Co. A, 32nd U. S. Infty.; and Indian Scouts. Major A. J. Alexander, 8th U. S. Cav., in command. Indians killed, 13.

October 10 .... Ft. Zarah, Kans. Lieut. August Kaiser, 3rd U. S. Infty., reported 8 horses and mules run off.

October 12 .... Near Ellsworth, Kans. Citizens killed, 1. Several missing.

October 12 .... Arkansas River, the Big Bend, Kans. Trs. H, K, and M, 7th U. S. Cav. Major J. H. Elliott in command. Indians killed, 2.

October 13-30 .... White Woman's Fork, near Republican River, Kans. Tr. H, 2nd U. S. Cav. Capt. Edward Ball in command. Indians killed, 2. Indians wounded, 3.

October 14 .... Sand Creek, Colo. Capt. W. H. Penrose, 3rd U. S. Infty., reported a train attacked. Led by "Satanta," chief of the Kiowas, a band of Indians ran off the cattle and captured 2 citizens, whom they later murdered.

October 14 .... Prairie Dog Creek, Kans. Tr. L. 5th U. S. Cav. Lieut. C. B. Brady in command. Soldiers killed, 1. Soldiers wounded, 1. Ran off 26 Cavalry horses.

October 15 .... Fisher and Yocucy Creeks, Kans. Citizens killed, 4. Soldiers wounded, 1. Citizens captured, 1.

October 18 .... Beaver Creek, Kans. Trs. H, I, and M, 10th U. S. Cav. Capt. L. H. Carpenter in command. Soldiers wounded, 3. Indians killed, 10.

October 19 .... Dragoon Fork of Verde River, Ariz. Tr. B, 8th U. S. Cav. Lieut. Rufus Somerby in command. Soldiers wounded, 1. Indians killed, 7.

October 21 .... Between Fts. Whipple and Verde, Ariz. Detachment of Tr. L, 8th U. S. Cav., and Detachment of Co. G, 14th U. S. Infty. Mail guard. Soldiers wounded, 1.

October 23 .... Ft. Zarah, Kans. Citizens killed, 2. Indians killed, 2.

October 25-26 .... Beaver Creek and Prairie Dog Creek, Kans. Trs. A, B, F, H, I, L. and M, 5th U. S. Cav., and Indian Scouts. Major E. A. Carr in command. Soldiers wounded, 1. Indians killed, 30. A number were wounded. 130 Indian ponies lost.

October 26 .... Central City, N. M. Citizens killed, 3.

October 26 .... Near Ft. Dodge, Kans. Co. E, 3rd U. S. Infty.

October 30 .... Grinnell Station, Kans. Indians wounded, 1.

November 2 .... Between Wickenberg and Prescott, Ariz. Detachment of Co. H, 14th U. S. Infty. Mail Escort. Soldiers killed, 1.

November 3 .... Big Coon Creek, Kans. Detachment of recruits, 7th U. S. Cav. Capt. F. W. Benteen in command.

November 7 .... Coon Creek, Kans. Attack on stage. One horse captured.

November 7-15 .... Scout from Willow Grove, Ariz. Detachments of Trs. E and K, 8th U. S. Cav. Major W. R. Price in command. Indians killed, 11. Indians wounded, 2. Indians captured, 20.

November 9-11 .... Tonto Plateaus, near Squaw Peak, Ariz. Detachments of Trs. B, and L, 8th U. S. Cav. Lieut. A. B. Wells in command. Soldiers wounded, 2. Indians killed, 15. Indians wounded, 40.

November 15 .... Near Ft. Harker, Kans. Squadron of 7th U. S. Cav. Indians wounded, 5.

November 17 .... Near Ft. Harker, Kans. Indians attacked a train. Ran off 150 mules.

November 18 .... Near Ft. Hays, Kans. Soldiers killed, 2. Indian scouts.

November 19 .... Near Ft. Dodge, Kans. Citizens killed, 1. Indians killed, 2.

November 19 .... Little Coon Creek, Kans. Citizens killed, 1. Indians killed, 5.

November 19 .... Near Ft. Dodge, Kans. Detachment of Tr. A, 10th U. S. Cav. Sergeant John Wilson in command. Indians killed, 2.

November 19 .... Near Ft. Dodge, Kans. Cos. A and H, 3rd U. S. Infty., and detachment of 5th U. S. Infty. Lieut. Quintin Campbell, 5th U. S. Infty., in command. Soldiers wounded, 3. Indians killed, 4. Indians wounded, 6.

November 20 .... Mulberry Creek, Kans. Government Scouts. Citizens killed, 2.

November 23 .... Southeast of Bill Williams Mountains, Ariz. Tr. B, 8th U. S. Cav. Capt. H. P. Wade in command. Indians killed, 2. Indians wounded, 1.

November 25-December 2 .... Scout from Camp McDowell, Ariz. Tr. I, 8th U. S. Cav.; Tr. E, 1st U. S. Cav.; and Co. A, 32nd U. S. Infty. Major A. J. Alexander, 8th U. S. Cav., in command. Soldiers wounded, 1. Indians killed, 2.

November 27 .... Black Kettles' Village, on Washita River, Indian Territory. Trs. A, B, C, D, E, F, G, H, I, K, and M, 7th U. S. Cav. Lieut. Col. Geo. A. Custer in command. Major J. H. Elliott and Capt. L. M. Hamilton killed. Lieut. T. W. Custer and Capts. Albert Barnitz and T. J. March, wounded. Soldiers killed, 19. Soldiers wounded, 13. Indians killed, 103. Indians captured, 53.

December 10 .... Walker Springs, Ariz. Trs. E and K, 8th U. S. Cav. Major W. R. Price in command. Indians killed, 3. Indians captured, 6.

December 11 .... Willow Grove, Ariz. Tr. K, 8th U. S. Cav. Major W. R. Price in command. Soldiers killed, 1. Indians killed, 8.

December 13 .... Walker Springs, Ariz. Trs. E and K, 8th U. S. Cav. Major W. R. Price in command. Indians killed, 8. Indians captured, 14.

December 25 .... Wichita Mountains, North Fork of Red River, Indian Territory. Trs. A, C, D, F, G, and I, 3rd U. S. Cav.; Cos. F and I, 37th U. S. Infty. Major A. W. Evans, 3rd U. S. Cav., in command. Indians killed, 25. Soldiers wounded, 3.

December 26 .... Near Ft. Cobb, Indian Territory. 7th U. S. Cav. Lieut. Col. Geo. A. Custer in command. Came upon a band of Kiowas. Took Satanta and Lone Wolf captive.

1869

January 8 .... Lake Station, Colo. Citizens killed, 2.

January 8-15 .... Scout in Bill Williams Mountains, Ariz. Trs. B and L, 8th U. S. Cav. Major D. R. Clendenin in command. Indians killed, 1.

January 13 .... Mount Turnbull, Ariz. Detachment of Tr. G, 1st U. S. Cav.; Detachment of Cos. F and G, 32nd U. S. Infty. Lieut. W. H. Winters, 1st U. S. Cav., in command. Indians killed, 1. Indians wounded, 1.

January 25 .... Kirkland's Creek, Juniper Mountains, Ariz. Trs. E, and K, 8th U. S. Cav. Capt. S. B. M. Young in command. Soldiers killed, 1.

January 28 .... Settlements on Solomon River, Kans. 7th U. S. Cav. Scouting party. Soldiers wounded, 2. Indians killed, 6. Indians captured, 10.

January 29 .... Mulberry Creek, Kans. Detachment of Trs. C, G, H, and K, 9th U. S. Cav. Capt. Edward Byrne in command. Soldiers wounded, 2. Indians killed, 6.

January 30 .... Saline River, Kans. Citizens killed, 2.

February 4 .... Arivaypa Mountains, Ariz. Detachments of Trs. G and K, 1st U. S. Cav.; Indian scouts. Capt. R. F. Bernard, 1st U. S. Cav., in command. Indians killed, 8. Indians captured, 8.

February 5 .... Black Mesa, Ariz. Detachment of Tr. L, 8th U. S. Cav. Indians killed, 1.

February 7 .... Ft. Selden, N. M. Troops from the Fort pursued Indians who had been stealing in the vicinity.

February 27 .... Near Camp Grant, Ariz. Detachment of Co. B, 14th U. S. Infty. Citizens killed, 2. Soldiers wounded, 1.

March 3 .... Oak Grove, Ariz. Detachment of Co. F, 32nd U. S. Infty. Indians killed, 1.

March 9 .... Ft. Harker, Kans. Indians with stolen stock overtaken by troops. Indians captured, 5.

March 13 .... Near Ft. Harker, Kans. Trs. A, B, C, D, E, F, G, H, I, K, and M. 7th U. S. Cav.

March 13 .... Shields River, Mont. Detachments of Cos. D, F, and G, 13th U. S. Infty. Capt. E. W. Clift in command. Citizens killed, 2. Indians killed, 4.

March 16 .... Near Ft. Randall, Dak. Detachments of Cos. C and F, 22nd U. S. Infty. Soldiers killed, 1.

March 17 .... Near Ft. Bayard, N. M. Apaches committed some murders and depredations. Troops pursued them to their village which they burned. Indians captured, 5.

March 17 .... Scouts from Camp Goodwin, Ariz. Detachments of Cos. B, F, and G, 32nd U. S. Infty. Capt. F. W. Perry in command. Indians killed, 2.

March 21 .... On San Carlos River, Ariz. 28 men of Tr. G, 1st U. S. Cav.; 10 men of Co. E, 32nd U. S. Infty.; 14 Indian Scouts; 6 Packers; 1 guide; and 1 hospital steward. Capt. R. F. Bernard, 1st U. S. Cav., in command. Two Indian women captured. Camp of 7 huts destroyed.

March 21 .... On headwaters of San Carlos River, Ariz. Two Indian children, two mules, camp of 37 huts captured by same expedition.

March 21 .... In Pinal Mountains, Ariz. Camp of 59 huts captured by same expedition.

March 22 .... Near Ft. Steele, Wyo. Detachments of Cos. A, B, F, H, and K, 30th U. S. Infty. Lieut. R. H. Young in command. Indians killed, 5.

March 23 .... Near Camp Grant, Ariz. Detachment of Co. E, 32nd U. S. Infty. Citizens killed, 1. Soldiers wounded, 2.

March 26 .... San Francisco Mountains, N. M. Detachment of Co. C, 38th U. S. Infty.

April 6 .... Near La Bonte Creek, Wyo. Detachment of Co. A, 4th U. S. Infty. Sergeant R. Rae in command. Soldiers killed, 2.

April 7 .... Musselshell River, Mont. Detachments of Cos. D, F, and G, 13th U. S. Infty. Capt. E. W. Clift in command. Soldiers killed, 1. Soldiers wounded, 2. Indians killed, 9.

April 14 .... Cienega, Ariz. Detachment of Co. E, 32nd U. S. Infty. Soldiers wounded, 2.

April 16 .... Near Ft. Wallace, Kans. Officer and escort.

April 20 .... Near Camp Crittenden, Ariz. Detachment of Co. H, 32nd U. S. Infty. Soldiers killed, 1.

April 20 .... Department of the Missouri. Troops pursued marauding Indians. Indians wounded, 3. Recovered 50 head of stolen stock.

April 22 .... Sangre Canyon, N. M. Trs. A, F, and H, 3rd U. S. Cav. Co. I. 37th U. S. Infty. On a Cavalry scouting party. Indians wounded, 5. Recovered 19 horses and a stolen check for $500.

April 29 .... Turnbull Mountain, Ariz. Detachments of Trs. C, G, and K, 1st U. S. Cav.; Co. B, 14th U. S. Infty., Co. I, 32nd U. S. Infty.; and Indian Scouts. Major John Green, 1st U. S. Cav., in command. Indians killed, 28. Indians captured, 8.

May 2 .... Near St. Augustine, N. M. Indians ambushed a train guarded by soldiers. Soldiers killed, 2. Soldiers wounded, 4. Indians killed, 5. Indians wounded, 10.

May 2-9 .... Scout in the Val de Chino Valley, Ariz. Detachment of Tr. L, 8th U. S. Cav. Lieut. A. B. Curtiss in command. Indians killed, 2.

May 6 .... Grief Hill, near Camp Verde, Ariz. Detachment of Tr. B, 8th U. S. Cav.; Co. C, 14th U. S. Infty. Train guard. Soldiers wounded, 5.

May 7 .... San Augustine Pass, N. M. Detachment of Tr. K, 3rd U. S.

Cav. Corporal C. Younge in command. Soldiers killed, 1. Soldiers wounded, 1. Citizens wounded, 1.

May 7 .... Paint Creek, near Double Mountain Fork, Texas. Detachments of Cos. E, and F, 35th U. S. Infty.; Indians scouts. Capt. G. W. Smith in command. Indians killed, 14.

May 10 .... Ft. Hays, Kans. Detachments of Cos. E, and G, 5th U. S. Infty. Attack of Indian prisoners on the guard. Soldiers killed, 1.

May 11 .... Near Ft. Lowell, Ariz. Detachment of Tr. G, 1st U. S. Cav.

May 13 .... Beaver Creek, or Elephant Rock, Kans. Trs. A, B, F, H, I, L, and M, 5th U. S. Cav. Major E. A. Carr in command. Soldiers killed, 4. Soldiers wounded, 3. Indians killed, 25. Indians wounded, 20.

May 15 .... Near Ft. Lowell, Ariz. Detachment of Tr. G, 1st U. S. Cav. Soldiers wounded, 1.

May 16 .... Spring Creek, Nebr. Trs. A, B, F, H, I, L, and M, 5th U. S. Cav. Major E. A. Carr in command. Fight was with 400 of the "Dog Soldier" Cheyennes. Soldiers wounded, 3.

May 18 .... Ft. Bayard, N. M. Indians ran off stock, were pursued by troops and their village destroyed.

May 18-26 .... Scout in Black Range, N. M. Detachment of Tr. B, 3rd U. S. Cav. Major H. C. Merriam, 38th U. S. Infty., in command.

May 21 .... Near Ft. Fred Steele, Wyo. Detachments of Co. B and H, 4th U. S. Infty. Lieut. J. H. Spencer in command.

May 22-28 .... Mineral Springs, vicinity of, Ariz. Tr. K, and Detachment of Tr. I, 1st U. S. Cav.; Co. I, 32nd U. S. Infty.; and Indian scouts. Capt. I. R. Dunkelberger, 1st U. S. Cav., in command. Indians killed, 4. Indians captured, 4. Skirmish with Apache Indians.

May 25 .... Settlements in Jewell County, Kans. Raided by the Indians. Citizens killed, 6.

May 26 .... Sheridan, Kans. Indians attacked a wagon train. Citizens wounded, 2.

May 29 .... Fossil Station, Kans. Citizens killed, 2. Citizens wounded, 4. At night threw a train from the track of the Kansas Pacific Railway.

May 30 .... Salt Creek, Kans. Citizens killed, 1. Attacked 3 couriers of the 7th U. S. Cav., and chased them 10 miles.

May 30 .... Near Ft. Hays, Kans. Attacked 3 government teamsters and drove them into the post.

May 30 to June 3 .... Near Toll Gate, Ariz. Detachment of Trs. E, F, and K, 8th U. S. Cav. Major W. R. Price in command. Indians killed, 4.

May 31 .... Rose Creek, Kans. A government train was attacked. Soldiers wounded, 2. Indians wounded, 5.

May 31 .... Buffalo Creek, Kans. Detachment of Tr. G, 7th U. S. Cav.

June 1 .... Settlements on Solomon River, Kans. Citizens killed, 13. 150 head of stock run off. Detachment of Cavalry pursued but without success.

June 1 .... Camp on Solomon River, Kans. Detachment of Tr. G, 7th

U. S. Cav. Soldiers wounded, 1. Indians wounded, 1. 3 Indian ponies captured.

June 3 ....Mineral Creek, Ariz. Tr. E, 1st U. S. Cav. Skirmish with Apache Indians.

June 3-4 .... Rio Pinto, Pinal Mountains, Ariz. Tr. E, 1st U. S. Cav.; Tr. C. 8th U. S. Cav.; Detachment of Co. F, 14th U. S. Infty. Capt. G. B. Sanford, 1st U. S. Cav., in command. Indians killed, 20. Indians captured, 4. Soldiers wounded, 1. Chief Squirrel Rifle killed.

June 4 .... Grinnell Station, Kans. Indians pulled up the track of the railroad but were repulsed by the military guard.

June 7 .... Johnson's River and Pecos River, Texas. Detachments of Trs. G, L, and M, 9th U. S. Cav. Col. R. S. Mackenzie, 41st U. S. Infty., in command. Soldiers killed, 1. Indians killed, 2.

June 10 .... Solomon River, Kans. Indians attempted to stampede the stock at the camp of a scouting party.

June 10 .... Settlements on Asher Creek, Kans. Town raided. Indians pursued by Cavalry. Stolen stock recovered.

June 11 .... Solomon River, Kans. Bat. A, 1st U. S. Artillery. Capt. W. M. Graham in command.

June 12 .... Solomon River, Kans. Some cavalry struck and pursued the trail of a marauding band of Indians, but did not succeed in over taking them.

June 16 .... Near Toll Gate, Ariz. Detachments of Trs. E and F, 8th U. S. Cav. Escort group under Lieut. A. B. Jerome. Soldiers killed, 1. Soldiers wounded, 1. Indians killed, 3.

June 19 .... Fort Wallace, Kans. Garrison Troops. Indians attacked a Government train. Detachments of Trs. B, C, and D, 5th U. S. Infty.

June 19 .... Near Sheridan, Kans. Detachment of Tr. E, 7th U. S. Cav. A surveying party, escorted by the cavalry, were attacked by Indians. Soldiers wounded, 2. Indians killed, 4. Indians wounded, 12.

June 19-July 5 .... Red Rock Country, Ariz. Tr. L, 8th U. S. Cav. Lieut. A. B. Curtiss in command. Indians killed, 7. Indians captured, 1.

June 20 .... Scandinavia, Kans. Detachment of Cavalry. Indians killed, 1.

June 26 .... Santa Maria River, near Toll Gate, Ariz. Tr. F, 8th U. S. Cav. Major W. R. Price in command. Indians killed, 4.

June 26 .... Sheridan, Kans. Soldiers killed, 1.

June 27 .... Great Mouth Canyon, Ariz. Tr. K, 8th U. S. Cav. Capt. S. B. M. Young in command. Indians killed, 3.

June 30 .... Burro Mountain, N. M. Tr. G, 1st U. S. Cav. Capt. R. F. Bernard in command. Indians wounded, 69. 4 mules captured. Fight with Cochise's band of Apache Indians.

July 3 .... Hell Canyon, Ariz. Tr. L, 8th U. S. Cav. Indians killed, 4. Lieut. A. B. Curtiss in command.

July 5 .... Frenchman's Fork, Colo. Trs. A, E, and M, 5th U. S. Cav.; Pawnee scouts. Major W. B. Royal, 5th U. S. Cav., in command. Indians killed, 3. Several Indians wounded.

July 6 .... Hac-qua-hallawater, Ariz. Detachment of Tr. E, 1st U. S.

Cav.; Detachment of Tr. C, 8th U. S. Cav. Lieut. Wm. Mc-Cleave, 8th U. S. Cav., in command. Soldiers wounded, 1. Indians killed, 9. Indians wounded, 10.

July 6 .... Frenchman's Fork, Nebr. Tr. A, 5th U. S. Cav. Lieut. G. F. Price in command. Indians killed, 3. Indians wounded, 3.

July 8 .... Near Republican River, Kans. Detachment of Tr. M, 5th U. S. Cav. Corporal John Kile in command. Indians wounded, 2.

July 8 .... Republican River, Kans. Night attack on Gen. Eugene A. Carr's camp. Soldiers wounded, 1.

July 10 to 17 .... New Mexico. Attacks on stages. Stages attacked 3 times in one week. Citizens killed, 10.

July 11 .... Summit Springs, Colo. Detachment of Trs. A, C, D, E, G, H, and M, 5th U. S. Cav.; and 3 companies of Indian scouts. Major E. A. Carr, 5th U. S. Cav., in command. Indian village was surprised and captured. 274 horses, 144 mules, quantities of arms and ammunition, and about $1,500 in United States money, were among the items captured. Soldiers wounded, 1. Indians killed, 52. Indians captured, 15. Chief Tall Bull killed.

July 13-August 19 .... Scout from Camp Grant, White Mountains, Ariz. Detachments of Trs. K and L, 1st U. S. Cav.; and Detachments of Cos. B, F, and I, 32nd U. S. Infty. Major John Green, 1st U. S. Cav., in command. Indians killed, 11. Indians wounded, 2. Indians captured, 13.

July 22-23 .... North Platte, Nebr. Tr. K, 2nd U. S. Cav. Lieut. J. A. Wanless in command. Soldiers wounded, 1.

July 25 .... Near Ft. Stanton, N. M. Troops struck the trail of Indians, pursued the savages to their village, destroyed it, Indians escaped into canyons. No casualties.

July 27 .... New Mexico. Troops pursued a band of Indians, overtaking them. Indians wounded, 3. Captured 3 Indian ponies and recovered some stolen stock.

August 2 .... Near Fort Sedgwick, Colo. Trs. A, C, D, E, G, H, and M, 5th U. S. Cav.; 3 companies of Pawnee scouts. Col. W. B. Royall, 5th U. S. Cav., in command.

August 3 .... Ft. Stevenson, Dak. Cos. E and F, 22nd U. S. Infty. Capt. S. A. Wainwright in command. Attack on herd.

August 5 .... Ft. Stevenson, Dak. Garrison of post and Detachment of scouts. Lieut. F. E. Parsons, 22nd U. S. Infty., in command. Co. R of the Scouts. Attack on herd.

August 9 .... Grinnell Station, Kans. Destroyed 150 yds. of telegraph line. Driven off by military guard.
Ft. Buford, Dak. Citizens killed, 4.

August 15 .... Near San Augustine Pass, N. M. Trs. F and H, 3rd U. S. Cav. Capt. Frank Stanwood in command.

August 19 .... Eagle Creek, Mont. Detachment of Co. B, 13th U. S. Infty. Train from Camp Cook, Mont. Citizens killed, 1. Indians killed, 4. Indians wounded, 2.

August 19 .... Near Helena, Mont. Citizens killed, 1. Citizens wounded, 1.

August 21 .... Cayote Station, Kans. Military guard.

August 25 .... Santa Maria River, Ariz. Tr. B, 8th U. S. Cav. Lieut. Rufus Somerby in command. Indians killed, 9. Indians wounded, 7.

August 25 .... Tonto Station, near Toll Gate, Ariz. Trs. E, F, and K, 8th U. S. Cav. Lieut. Robert Carrick in command. Indians killed, 6. Indians captured, 1.

August 26 .... Tonto Pleateau, near Toll Gate, Ariz. Trs. E, F, and K, 8th U. S. Cav. Lieut. Robert Carrick in command. Soldiers killed, 1.

September 5 .... Troops from Ft. Stanton, N. M. Soldiers wounded, 2. Soldiers killed, 3. Soldiers wounded, 7.

September 5 .... Camp Date Creek, Ariz. Tr. B, 8th U. S. Cav.; Detachment of Co. F, 12th U. S. Infty. Lieut. Rufus Somerby in command. Indians killed, 3.

September 12 .... Laramie Peak, Wyo. Detachments of Cos. D and G, 4th U. S. Infty. Lieut. T. E. True in command. Soldiers killed, 1. Soldiers wounded, 1. Train escort.

September 14 .... Popo Agie, Wyo. Tr. D, 2nd U. S. Cav. Lieut. C. B. Stambaugh in command. Soldiers wounded, 2. Indians killed, 2. Indians wounded, 7.

September 14 .... Little Wind River, Wyo. One man of Co. K, 7th U. S. Infty. The man was John Holt and he was killed.

September 14 .... On Popoagie River, Wyo. Detachment of Tr. D, 2nd U. S. Cav. Lieut. C. B. Stambaugh in command. Soldiers killed, 2. Indians killed, 2. Indians wounded, 10. One Indian pony captured.

September 15 .... Near Whiskey Gap, Wyo. Detachment of Co. B, 4th U. S. Infty.; and Cos. B, D, F, and I, 7th U. S. Infty. Lieut. J. H. Spencer, 4th U. S. Infty., in command. Soldiers killed, 1. Fight with about 300 Indians.

September 16 .... Salt Fork of Brazos River, Texas. Trs. B, C, F, and M, 9th U. S. Cav.; Detachment of 41st U. S. Infty. Capt. Henry Carroll, 9th U. S. Cav., in command. Soldiers wounded, 3

September 17 .... Near Ft. Stanton, N. M. Indians ran off stock, were pursued, their village destroyed. Indians wounded, 3.

September 17 .... Point of Rocks, Wyo. Attack on stage. Citizens killed, 1.

September 17 .... Twin Creek, Wyo. Mail escort attacked and driven into the mountains.

September 20-21 .... Brazos River, Texas. Detachments of Tr. B and E, 9th U. S. Cav. Capt. Henry Carroll in command. Soldiers wounded, 1.

September 20 .... Ft. Bascom, N. M. Troops from fort pursued a band of Indians into the mountains.

September 23 .... Red Creek, Ariz. Cos. D and L, 8th U. S. Cav. Lieut. T. W. Gibson in command. Indians killed, 18.

September 23 .... Ft. Cummings, N. M. Troops from the Fort pursued marauding Indians and recaptured 30 stolen horses.

September 24 .... Ranches near Ft. Bayard, N. M. Troops followed Indians to their village and destroyed it. Indians wounded, 3.

September 26 .... San Francisco Mountains, N. M. Troops pursued

Indians to their village, destroyed it, and recovered some stolen sheep. Indians wounded, 2.

September 26 .... Prairie Dog Creek, Kans. Trs. B, C, F, L, and M, 5th U. S. Cav.; Trs. B, C, and M, 2nd U. S. Cav.; and 2 companies of Pawnee scouts. Lieut. Col. Thos. Duncan, 5th U. S. Cav., in command. Indians killed, 1. Indians captured, 1. Pursued the Indians to their village, consisting of 56 lodges, which was destroyed the following day. From the Indian prisoner it was ascertained that the band were all Sioux, under Pawnee Killer and Whistler. Some surveyor's instruments were also found and identified as belonging to Mr. Nelson Buck's surveying party, consisting of about 12 persons, all of whom had been recently murdered and their camp destroyed.

September 29 .... Near Ft. Bayard, N. M. Post troops pursued the Indians for a week, destroyed their village. Soldiers wounded, 1. Indians killed, 3. Indians wounded, 3.

September 29-October 6 .... Mimbres Mountains, N. M. Detachment of Tr. B, 3rd U. S. Cav., and Cos. A and C, 38th U. S. Infty.

October 5 .... Dragoon Springs, Ariz. Detachment of Co. D, 21st U. S. Infty. Soldiers killed, 4.

October 8 .... Chiricahua Pass, Ariz. Detachment of Tr. G, 1st U. S. Cav. Lieut. W. H. Winters in command. Soldiers wounded, 2. Indians killed, 12. Fight was with Apache Indians.

October 12 .... Red Rock, Ark. Tr. L, 8th U. S. Cav. Non-commissioned officer in command. Indians killed, 2.

October 15 .... Mogollon Mountains, N. M. Troops pursued a band of Indians to the mountains and recaptured 30 horses.

October 20 .... Chiricahua Mountains, Ariz. Tr. G, 1st U. S. Cav. and Tr. G, 8th U. S. Cav. Capt. R. F. Bernard, 1st U. S. Cav., in command. Soldiers killed, 2. Lieut. John Lafferty, 8th U. S. Cav., wounded. Soldiers wounded, 2. Indians killed, 18. Fight was with Apache Indians.

October 23 .... Mimbres Mountains, N. M. Troops pursued Indians to mountains where they defeated them. Soldiers wounded, 1. Indians killed, 3. Indians wounded, 3.

October 27 .... In Chiricahua Mountains, Ariz. Tr. G, 1st U. S. Cav.; Tr. G, 8th U. S. Cav. Capt. R. F. Bernard in command. Fight with Cochise's band of Chiricahua Apaches.

October 28-29 .... Headwaters of Brazos River, Texas. Trs. B, C, F, G, L, and M, 9th U. S. Cav.; Trs. D and F, 4th U. S. Cav.; Detachment of 24th U. S. Infty.; and Indian Scouts. Capt. J. M. Bacon, 9th U. S. Cav., in command. Soldiers wounded, 8. Indians killed, 50. Indians captured, 7.

October 31 .... Chiricahua Mountains, Ariz. Tr. G, 8th U. S. Cav.; and Trs. C and G, 1st U. S. Cav. Capt. R. F. Bernard, 1st U. S. Cav., in command. Indians killed, 2.

November 2 .... Near Ft. Sill, Indian Territory. Troops recovered a white captive from a band of Indians.

November 6 .... Garde, Ariz. Tr. K, 8th U. S. Cav. Lieut. J. D. Stevenson in command. Indians captured, 2.

November 6 .... Between Fts. Fetterman and Laramie, Wyo. Tr. K,

2nd U. S. Cav. Capt. James Egan in command. Soldiers killed, 2.

November 10 .... Tompkins Valley, Ariz. Tr. L, 8th U. S. Cav. Non-commissioned officer in command. Indians killed, 4.

November 16-28 .... Scout on Santa Maria River, Ariz. Detachment of Trs. D and L, 8th U. S. Cav. Capt. Chas. Hobart in command. Indians wounded, 2. Indians killed, 2.

November 18 .... Guadaloupe Mountains, N. M. Detachment of Tr. F, 3rd U. S. Cav. Lieut. H. B. Cushing in command. Pursued Indians 200 miles. Soldiers wounded, 2. Indians captured, 1. Recovered 150 head of stolen stock.

November 24 .... Headwaters of Llano River, Texas. Detachments of Trs. F and M, 9th U. S. Cav. Capt. E. M. Heyl in command. Capt. Heyl wounded. Indians killed, 1.

December 1 .... Near Horseshoe, Wyo. Detachments of Cos. A, D, E, F, G, and K, 4th U. S. Infty. Mail escort. Sergeant Conrad Bahr, Co. E, in command. Soldiers wounded, 3.

December 2 .... Between Ft. Laramie and Ft. Fetterman, Wyo. Mail escort of ten men attacked. Soldiers wounded, 2.

December 10 .... Mount Buford, or Chilson's Creek, Ariz. Detachment of Tr. G, 1st U. S. Cav.; Tr. A, 8th U. S. Cav. Capt. G. B. Sanford, 1st U. S. Cav., in command. Soldiers wounded, 1. Indians killed, 11. Fight with Apache Indians.

December 9-10 .... Walnut Hill, Lee County, Va. Detachment of Tr. K, 5th U. S. Cav.

December 15 .... Bunker Hill Station, Kans. Indians attacked but were repulsed by military guard.

December 16 .... Pinto Creek, Ariz. Tr. K, 1st U. S. Cav.; Trs. C and I, 8th U. S. Cav. Capt. Wm. Kelley, 8th U. S. Cav., in command. Killed several Indians and captured their women and children.

December 25 .... Johnson's Mail Station, Texas. Detachment of Tr. E, 9th U. S. Cav. Non-commissioned officer in command.

December 26 .... Sanguinara Canyon, Guadaloupe Mountains, Texas. Tr. F, 3rd U. S. Cav. Lieut. H. B. Cushing in command. Lieut. Franklin Yeaton severly wounded and later died.

December 26 .... Ft. Wrangel, Alaska. Bat. I, 2nd U. S. Artillery. Lieut. Wm. Borrows in command. Citizens wounded, 1. Indians killed, 2. Indians wounded, 1.

December 30 .... Delaware Creek, Guadaloupe Mountains, Texas. Tr. F, 3rd U. S. Cav. Lieut. H. B. Cushing in command.

1870

January 3-February 6 .... Scout on Rio Grande and Pecos Rivers, Texas. Tr. G, and Detachment of Tr. L, 9th U. S. Cav.; Detachments of Cos. L, and K, 24th U. S. Infty. Capt. J. M. Bacon, 9th U. S. Cav., in command.

January 6 .... Guadaloupe Mountains, Texas. Tr. H, 9th U. S. Cav.

January 11 .... Lower Pecos River, Texas. Tr. L, 9th U. S. Cav. Lieut. Chas. Parker in command. Indians killed, 1.

January 13-February 3 .... North of Gila River, Ariz. Detachments of Trs. K and M, 1st U. S. Cav.

January 16 .... Indian Village, Texas. Tr. G, and Detachment of Tr. L, 9th U. S. Cav.

January 20 .... Delaware Creek, Guadalupe Mountains, Texas. Detachments of Trs. C, D, I, and K, 9th U. S. Cav. Capt. F. S. Dodge in command. Soldiers wounded, 2.

January 23 .... Piegan Camp, Marias River, Mont. Action with Blackfeet Indians at camps of Bear Chief and Big Horn. Trs. F, G, H, and L, 2nd U. S. Cav.; Cos. A, F, I, and K, 13th U. S. Infty. Major E. M. Baker, 2nd U. S. Cav., in command. Soldiers killed, 2. Indians killed, 175. Indians wounded, 40. Indians captured, 140. Burned the camp of Mountain Chief. Troops marched for the Northwest Fur Cos. Station, arriving January 25. Col. Baker sent for the chiefs of the Bloods and asked them to give up all stolen stock. The column reached Ft. Ellis February 6 after a march of about 600 miles.

January 27 .... Dragoon Mountains, Ariz. Tr. G, 1st U. S. Cav.; detachment of Tr. G, 8th U. S. Cav. Capt. R. F. Bernard, 1st U. S. Cav., in command. Indians killed, 13. Indians captured 2. Fight with Cochise's band of Apaches.

January 28 .... Dragoon Mountains, Ariz. Same force destroyed Camp of Cochise, Chiricahua Apache Chief.

March 9 .... Reno Road, near Camp McDowell, Ariz. Detachment of Tr. I, 8th U. S. Cav. Sergt Francis Brannon in command. Soldiers wounded, 1. Citizens wounded, 1. Indians killed, 4.

March 15-16 .... Vicinity of Sol's Wash, Ariz. Detachment of Co. H, 21st U. S. Infty. Lieut. J. F. Cluley in command. Indians killed, 2.

March 21 .... Eagle Tail Station, Kans. Indians attacked a railroad working party, but were driven off by the military guards; no casualties.

April 2 .... Headwaters of Sweetwater, Wyo. Citizens killed, 6.

April 3 .... San Martine Springs, Texas. Detachment of Tr. H, 9th U. S. Cav. Non-commissioned officer in command. Indians killed, 1.

April 3 .... North Hubbard Creek, Texas. Detachment of Tr. F, 4th U. S. Cav. Capt. Wirt Davis in command. Indians killed, 2. Indians wounded, 4.

April 6 .... Bluff Creek, Kans. Train escort. Indians wounded, 3. 130 miles stampeded.

April 6 .... Near Clear Creek, Texas. Detachment of Tr. M, 10th U. S. Cav. Lieut. W. R. Harmon in command. Indians killed, 1. Indian captured, 10.

April 23 .... Kansas. A railroad working party were attacked by Indians, who were repulsed by the military guards. No casualties.

April 25 .... Crow Springs, Texas. Detachments of Trs. C, and K, 9th U. S. Cav. Major A. P. Morrow in command.

April 30 .... Pinal Mountains, near San Carlos, Ariz. Detachment of Tr. E, 1st U. S. Cav.; Detachment of Tr. B, 3rd U. S. Cav.; and Detachment of 21st U. S. Infty. Capt. G. B. Sanford, 1st

U. S. Cav., in command. Indians killed, 11. Indians captured, 4.

May 4 .... Miner's Delight, near Twin Creek, Wyo. Tr. D, 2nd U. S. Cav. Capt. D. S. Gordon in command. Lieut. C. B. Stambaugh, 2nd U. S. Cav., killed. Soldiers wounded, 1. Indians killed, 7. Indians wounded, 1.

May 14 .... Mount Adams, Texas. Detachment of Tr. M, 4th U. S. Cav. Lieut. Wm. Russell, Jr., in command. Lieut. Russell, Jr., mortally wounded. Soldiers wounded, 2.

May 16 .... Kansas Pacific Railroad. Indians made a concerted attack along the railroad for a distance of 30 miles, killing 10 persons and running off about 300 animals. A troop of Cavalry pursued the Indians to the Republican River, Nebr., but without success.

May 17 .... Spring Creek, or Little Blue, Nebr. Detachment of Tr. C, 2nd U. S. Cav. Sergt. P. Leonard in command. Soldiers wounded, 1. Indians killed, 1. Indians wounded, 7. Sergt. Leonard and 4 men of Tr. C, 2nd Cav., while searching for strayed horses, were suddenly surrounded and fired upon by a party of 50 Indians. Private Hubbard and 2 horses wounded at first fire. Sergeant turned horses over to Hubbard. Indians repulsed. Sergeant killed the 2 wounded horses and formed a breastwork of them. Indians again charged. Kept it up for 2 hours and retired. Sergeant took in charge a Settlers family and made his way to Capt. Spaulding's camp.

May 18 .... Lake Station, Colo. Indians attacked the station and were pursued by a party of cavalry but without success.

May 19-20 .... Kickapoo Springs, Texas. Detachment of Tr. F, 9th U. S. Cav. Sergt. E. Stance in command. Indians wounded, 4.

May 21 .... Hugo Station, Colo. Was attacked by Indians, who were repulsed.

May 25 .... Tonto Valley, Ariz. Tr. E, 1st U. S. Cav.; Tr. E, 3rd U. S. Cav. Capt. G. B. Sanford, 1st U. S. Cav., in command. Indians killed, 21. Indians captured, 12.

May 28 .... Near Camp Supply, Indian Territory. Citizens killed, 2. Indians attacked a train, stampeded all the mules and killed one man. The same day they ran off a quantity of stock near the post and killed another man.

May 29 .... Bass Canyon, Texas. Tr. K, 9th U. S. Cav. Lieut. I. W. Trask in command. Soldiers killed, 1.

May 29-June 26 .... Near Camp Apache, Ariz. Detachment of Tr. A, 3rd U. S. Cav. Capt. Wm. Hawley in command. Indians wounded, 1. Indians captured, 6.

May 30 .... Holiday Creek, Texas. Detachments of Trs. C and D, 9th U. S. Cav. Lieut. I. N. Walter in command. Soldiers killed, 1. Citizens wounded, 2.

May 31 .... Carlyle Station, Kans. Attacked by Indians. They were repulsed by the military guard. Soldiers wounded, 2. Indians wounded, 3.

May 31 .... Bear Creek, Kans. Detachments of Cos. B, and F, 3rd U. S. Infty. Mail guard. Sergt. James Murray in command.

Soldiers killed, 2. Soldiers wounded, 1. Indians killed, 5. Indians captured, 10.

June 1 .... Solomon River, Kans. Tr. M, 7th U. S. Cav. Settlements raided and Indians pursued by Cavalry. Indians wounded, 4.

June 2 .... Near Copper Canyon, Ariz. Detachment of Co. C, 21st U. S. Infty. Post guard. Soldiers killed, 1. Indians killed, 1.

June 3 .... Near Ft. Whipple, Ariz. Detachment of Tr. M, 3rd U. S. Cav. Lieut. J. C. Graham in command. Soldiers killed, 2.

June 3 .... Department of the Missouri. A Mexican was killed and scalped. A train was attacked, a teamster killed, and 40 mules stampeded, and Capt. Armes, 10th U. S. Cav., being separated from his escort, was attacked and chased, but escaped.

June 5 .... Apache Mountains, Ariz. Detachment of Tr. K, 1st U. S. Cav.; and Detachments of Trs. B and F, 3rd U. S. Cav. Lieut. H. B. Cushing, 3rd U. S. Cav., in command. Indians killed, 30.

June 5 .... Black Canyon, Ariz. Detachment of Tr. M, 3rd U. S. Cav. Lieut. J. C. Graham in command. Indians killed, 2.

June 6 .... Near Ft. Selden, N. M. The chief engineer officer, District of New Mexico, whilst surveying near that post, was attacked and two mules captured. Troops from the post pursued the Indians who, however, escaped.

June 6 .... Near Camp Supply, Indian Territory. An attack on a train was repulsed. At night the Indians again attacked the train and were driven off. They captured 13 mules. Two Indians were wounded.

June 8 .... Between Ft. Dodge, Kans., and Camp Supply, Indian Territory. Trs. F and H, 10th U. S. Cav. Lieut. J. A. Bodamer in command. Soldiers wounded, 2. Indians killed, 3.

June 8 .... Red Willow Creek, Nebr. Tr. I, 5th U. S. Cav. Lieut. E. D. Thomas in command. Indians killed, 3.

June 8 .... Near Camp Supply, Indian Territory. United States mail escort attacked by Indians. Indians killed, 3. Indians wounded, 5. Soldiers wounded, 1.

June 8 .... Near Camp Supply, Indian Territory. Government train, guarded by a troop of cavalry, was attacked by Indians. Soldiers wounded, 3. Indians killed, 3. Indians wounded, 10.

June 10 .... Snake Creek, Indian Territory. Tr. H, 10th U. S. Cav. Capt. L. H. Carpenter in command.

June 11 .... Camp Supply, Indian Territory. Trs. A, F, G, I, and K, 9th U. S. Cav.; Cos. B, E, and F, 3rd U. S. Infty. Lieut. Col. A. D. Nelson, 3rd U. S. Infty., in command. Indians killed, 6. Indians wounded, 10.

June 11 .... Near Bunker Hill Station, Kans. Cavalry couriers carrying dispatches were attacked and chased into the station.

June 11 .... Near Grinnell Station, Kans. A train escorted by cavalry was attacked by Indians, who were repulsed after a fight of 3 hours; no casualties.

June 13 .... Ft. Buford, Dakota. Cos. C, E, and H, 13th U. S. Infty.

Lieut. Col. H. A. Morrow in command. Citizens wounded, 4. Indians killed, 1.

June 13 .... Grinnell, Kans. Detachment of Tr. M, 7th U. S. Cav. Indians attacked a railroad working party. Indians killed, 3. Indians wounded, 10.

June 14 .... Republican River, Kans. Battalion of 7th U. S. Cav. Encountered a band of Indians. The advance troop attacked the Indians who, however, escaped with a loss of one pony killed.

June 15 .... Near Ft. Bascom, N. M. Indians plundered a ranch. Citizens killed, 1. Five horses stolen. Indians fired upon by guard but escaped.

June 15 .... East branch of Rio Verde, Ariz. Tr. E, 3rd U. S. Cav. Capt. Alex. Sutorius in command.

June 16 .... Mulberry Creek, Kans. Indians killed three wood-choppers.

June 18 .... North Platte, Nebr. Tr. E, 2nd U. S. Cav. Capt. E. R. Wells in command. Indians wounded, 1.

June 21 .... Near Carson, Colo. Indians attacked a Mexican train and killed five teamsters. Cavalry pursued next day, but without success.

June 24 .... White Mountains, Ariz. Detachments of Trs. A, C, L, and M, 3rd U. S. Cav. Capt. Wm. Hawley in command. Soldiers wounded, 3. Indians killed, 1. Indians captured, 7.

June 25 .... Medicine Bow Station, Wyo. Detachment of Tr. I, 2nd U. S. Cav. Lieut. C. T. Hall in command.

June 27 .... Pine Grove Meadow, Wyo. Detachment of Tr. A, 2nd U. S. Cav. Lieut. R. H. Young, 4th U. S. Infty., in command. Soldiers wounded, 1. Indians killed, 15. Attacked a band of 200 Indians.

June 27 .... Calamus River, Nebr. Detachment of Tr. K, 2nd U. S. Cav. Lieut. E. C. Bartlett in command. Indians killed, 1.

July 12 .... Near North Fork, Little Wichita River, Texas. Detachments of Trs. A, C, D, H, K, and L, 6th U. S. Cav. Capt. C. B. McLellan in command. Soldiers killed, 2. Soldiers wounded, 6. Citizens wounded, 1. Indians killed, 15. Acting Assistant Surgeon G. W. Hatch wounded.

July 14 .... Near Mount Paso, Texas. Detachment of Trs. D and F, 4th U. S. Cav. Capt. Wirt Davis in command. Indians killed, 1.

July 25 .... Pinal Mountains, Ariz. Tr. F, 3rd U. S. Cav. Lieut. H. B. Cushing in command.

August .... Washita River, Indian Territory. Detachment of Cavalry. Soldiers killed, 2. Soldiers wounded, 5. Indians killed, 3. Indians wounded, 10.

August 1 .... Skirmish Canyon, Apache Mountains, Ariz. Tr. F, 3rd U. S. Cav.; Tr. K, 1st U. S. Cav. Lieut. H. B. Cushing, 3rd U. S. Cav., in command. Soldiers killed, 1. Indians killed, 6.

August 1 .... Pinal Mountains, Ariz. 25 men of Tr. K, 1st U. S. Cav. Sergt. Taylor in command. Indians killed, 6. Blacksmith Joseph Graff of Tr. K, was killed in the action. Fight with the Apache Indians.

August 10 .... Staked Plain, N. M. Tr. D, 8th U. S. Cav. Lieut. H. S.
Weeks in command. Indians captured, 2.
August 18 .... Mescal Ranch, Ariz. Detachment of Co. D, 21st U. S.
Infty. Mail Escort. Soldiers killed, 2. Citizens killed, 1.
August 22 .... Near Camp McDowell, Ariz. Detachment of Tr. E,
1st U. S. Cav. Capt. G. B. Sanford in command. Indians
killed, 1.
September 30 .... Near Ft. Concho, Texas. Detachment of Tr. E,
4th U. S. Cav. Mail Escort. Soldiers killed, 1.
October 1 .... Yellowstone River, Dak. Indians scouts from Ft. Bu-
ford. Lieut. W. H. Nelson, 7th U. S. Infty., in command.
October 5 .... Little Wichita River (near), Texas Tr. M, 6th U. S.
Cav., and Indian Scouts. Capt. W. A. Rafferty in command.
Indians killed, 2. Indians wounded, 1.
October 6 .... Looking Glass, or Shell Creek, Nebr. Tr. K, 2nd U. S.
Cav. Capt. James Egan in command. Indians killed, 1.
October 6 .... Pinal Mountains, Ariz. Tr. F, 3rd U. S. Cav. Lieut. H.
B. Cushing in command. Soldiers wounded, 2. Indians kill-
ed, 2.
October 6 .... Near Little Wichita River, Texas. Tr. G, 6th U. S.
Cav. Capt. T. C. Tupper in command.
October 16 .... Guadaloupe Mountains, N. M. Tr. A and B, 8th U. S.
Cav. Capt. Wm. McCleave in command. Indians captured,
9.
October 29 .... Pinal Mountains, Ariz. Tr. C, 1st U. S. Cav. Capt.
Harrison Moulton in command. Soldiers wounded, 2. In-
dians killed, 4.
October 30 .... Near Ft. Stanton, N. M. Indians stampeded 59 mules
from a train. Cavalry pursued for 255 miles, destroyed the
Indian village, recovered the mules, captured 3 squaws.
October 31-November 22 .... Guadalupe Mountains, N. M. Detach-
ment of Tr. A, 8th U. S. Cav.
November 14 .... Scout from Ft. Richardson, Texas. Detachment of
Tr. I, 6th U. S. Cav. Capt. A. R. Chaffee in command.
November 18 .... Lowell Station, Kans. Citizens killed, 1.
November 19 .... Near Carson, Colo. Indians stampeded 68 mules
from a Mexican train.
November .... In the Guadaloupe Mountains, N. M. Detachment of
Tr. A, 8th U. S. Cav. Lieut. Pendleton Hunter in command.
Indians captured, 9.
December 14 .... Turnbull Mountains, Ariz. Tr. F, 3rd U. S. Cav.
Lieut. H. B. Cushing in command.

1871

January 1 .... Pinal Mountains, near Gila River, Ariz. Tr. G, and De-
tachments of Tr. K, 1st U. S. Cav.; and Tr. H, 3rd U. S. Cav.
Tr. G, 8th U. S. Cav. Capt. R. F. Bernard, 1st U. S. Cav., in
command. Indians killed, 9.
January 7 .... Cienega, near Camp Verde, Ariz. Detachments of
Trs. A, E, and G, 3rd U. S. Cav. Lieut. G. W. Cradlebaugh in
command. Acting Assistant Surgeon A. G. Steigers wound-
ed. Citizens wounded, 1.
January 9 .... East Fork River, near Mazatzal Mountains, Ariz. Capt.
Wm. Hawley in command.

February 12 .... Chiricahua Mountains, Ariz. Tr. C, 8th U. S. Cav. Capt. Wm. Kelly in command. Indians killed, 14. Indians wounded, 20. Indians captured, 1.

February 13 .... Sierra Galiero, Ariz. Tr. F, 3rd U. S. Cav. Lieut. H. B. Cushing in command.

February 14 .... Arivaypa Mountains, Ariz. Tr. F, 3rd U. S. Cav. Lieut. H. B. Cushing in command.

February 17 .... Near Ft. Bayard, N. M. Indians raided the ranches, murdered the settlers and ran off stock. Troops pursued the Indians to the mountains, burned their village, destroyed its contents and recovered many of the stolen animals. Soldiers killed, 1. Soldiers wounded, 2. Indians killed, 14. Indians wounded, 20.

February 26 .... Near Grinnell, Kans. Indians attacked a hunter's camp, burned it, and ran off the stock.

March 18 .... Near Ft. Dodge, Kans. Indians made repeated attacks upon a government train. Soldiers killed, 3. Indians wounded, 5.

March 21 .... Paloncillo Mountains, Ariz. Detachment of Tr. K, 3rd U. S. Cav. Capt. Gerald Russell in command. Indians wounded, 3.

March 28 .... Gila River, near Gila Mountains, Ariz. Detachment of Tr. K, 3rd U. S. Cav. Capt. Gerald Russell in command. Soldiers wounded, 1. Indians wounded, 15.

April 1—3 .... Near Date Creek, Ariz. Detachment of Tr. B, 3rd U. S. Cav. Lieut. J. A. Haughey, 21st U. S. Infty., in command.

April 4 .... Sierra Aniba, Ariz. Tr. F, 3rd U. S. Cav. Lieut. H. B. Cushing in command. Indians killed, 1.

April 11 .... Apache Mountains, Ariz. Tr. F, 3rd U. S. Cav. Lieut. H. B. Cushing in command. Indians killed, 4. Indians captured, 2.

April 12 .... Apache Mountains, Ariz. Tr. F, 3rd U. S. Cav. Lieut. H. B. Cushing in command. Indians killed, 27.

April 16 .... Dragoon Mountains, Ariz. Detachment of Tr. K, 3rd U. S. Cav. Capt. Gerald Russell in command.

April 27 .... Ft. Sill, Indian Territory. Detachment of Tr. E, 10th U. S. Cav. Lieut. S. L. Woodward in command. Indians captured, 1.

April 30 .... Colorado. Apache Indians from Arizona attacked settlers. Citizens killed, 20.

May 3 .... Near Cimarron, N. M. Indians raided the settlements. Citizens killed, 3. Ran off about 950 head of stock. Troops pursued, captured 22 Indians, and recovered 757 head of stolen stock.

May 5 .... Whetstone Mountains, Ariz. Detachment of Tr. F, 3rd U. S. Cav. Lieut. H. B. Cushing in command. Lieut. Cushing killed. Soldiers killed, 1. Soldiers wounded, 1. Indians killed, 13.

May 11 .... New Mexico. Major Wm. R. Price with a squadron of the 8th U. S. Cav. pursued a band of marauding Navajoes in New Mexico, captured two prominent chiefs and recovered a large number of stolen animals.

May 12 .... Near Red River, Texas. Detachment of Tr. L, 10th U. S. Cav. Indians ran off stock. Citizens killed, 7. Indians killed, 3. Indians wounded, 4.

May 15 .... New Mexico. Indians stampeded 22 mules from a government train.

May 15 .... Near Camp Apache, Ariz. Detachment of Trs. L and M, 1st U. S. Cav. Fight with Apache Indians.

May 17 .... Ft. Sill, Indian Territory. Trs. B, D, E, and H, 10th U. S. Cav. Soldiers wounded, 1. Indians killed, 1. Indians captured, 2. Indians went to Fort Sill where they publicly avowed the deeds of May 12 in the presence of Gen. Sherman and the Post Commander. The Chiefs "Satanta" and "Big Tree" arrested. Followers resisted. Chief "Satank" killed.

May 20 .... Brazos and Big Wishita Divide, Texas. Tr. A, 4th U. S. Cav. Lieut. P. M. Boehm in command. Soldiers wounded, 1. Indians killed, 1.

May 21 .... Camp Melvin Station, Texas. Detachment of Tr. K, 25th U. S. Infty. Sergt. J. Walker in command. Soldiers wounded, 2.

May 24 .... Birdwood Creek, Nebr. Detachments of Trs. G, H, I, and L, 5th U. S. Cav. Lieut. E. M. Hayes in command. Indians captured, 6.

May 28 .... Canadian Mountains, Texas. Tr. D, 8th U. S. Cav. Capt. J. F. Randlett in command. Indians captured, 12. Capture of traders.

May 29 .... Kiowa Springs, N. M. Tr. F, 8th U. S. Cav. Lieut. A. P. Caraher in command. Indians captured, 22. Capture of traders and cattle thieves.

May 29 .... Department of the Missouri. Cavalry pursued a band of Indians and recaptured 500 stolen animals.

June 1 .... Huachuca Mountains, Ariz. Tr. F, 3rd U. S. Cav. Capt. Alex. Moore in command. Indians killed, 3.

June 8—9 .... East Fork of Verde River, Mazatzal Mountains, and Wild Rye Creek, Ariz. (Running fight). Detachments of Trs. A, D, and G, 3rd U. S. Cav. Lieut. Chas. Morton in command. Indians killed, 56. Indians wounded, 8.

June 10 .... Huachuca Mountains, Ariz. Tr. F, 3rd U. S. Cav. Capt. Alex. Moore in command.

June 26 .... Camp Brown, Wyo. Detachment of Tr. B, 2nd U. S. Cav.; Detachment of Co. A, 13th U. S. Infty. Sergt. N. F. Cheeney, Tr. B, 2nd U. S. Cav., in command.

June 28 .... Pawnee Fork, Kans. Indians ran off 24 horses. Stole 70 mules.

June 30 .... Staked Plains, Texas. Detachment of Tr. I, 9th U. S. Cav.; Detachment of the 24th U. S. Infty. Lieut. Col. W. R. Shafter, 24th U. S. Infty., in command. Indians captured, 1.

July .... Between Fts. Apache and McDowell, Ariz. Capt. G. V. Henry, 3rd U. S. Cav., in command. Indians killed, 7. Indians captured, 11.

July 2 .... Ft. Larned, Kans. Cos. C and E, 3rd U. S. Infty. Attacked by the Indians, but repulsed by the troops.

July 4 .... Bandaro Pass, Texas. Detachment of Tr. M, 4th U. S.

Cav. Sergt. D. Harrington in command. Indians wounded, 2.

July 13 .... Cienega de Los Pinos, Ariz. Co. G, 21st U. S. Infty. Capt. H. M. Smith in command. Soldiers killed, 1. Soldiers wounded, 3. Indians killed, 15.

July 15 .... Double Mountain Fork of Brazos River, Texas. Detachment of Tr. G, 4th U. S. Cav. Lieut. W. C. Hemphill in command.

July 19 .... Bear Springs, near Camp Bowie, Ariz. Detachment of Tr. K, 3rd U. S. Cav. Lieut. G. A. Drew in command. Citizens killed, 2. Soldiers wounded, 1.

July 22 .... Headwaters of Concho River, Texas. One man of Tr. F, 9th U. S. Cav. Soldiers wounded, 1.

July 31 .... Near McKavett, Texas. Detachment of Tr. M, 9th U. S. Cav., and Detachment of Co. A, 24th U. S. Infty. Capt. F. M. Crandal, 24th U. S. Infty., in command. Indians killed, 1.

August 18 .... Near Ft. Stanton, N. M. Citizens killed, 1. Killed a settler and ran off his stock. Troops pursued, but without success.

August 25 .... Arivaypa Canon, Ariz. Tr. H, 3rd U. S. Cav. Capt. Frank Stanwood in command. Indians killed, 5.

September 1 .... Near Ft. McKavett, Texas Detachment of Tr. M, 9th U. S. Cav. and Co. E, 24th U. S. Infty. Capt. J. W. Clous, 24th U. S. Infty., in command.

September 5 .... Chino Valley, Ariz. Citizens killed, 1.

September 13 .... Near Tucson, Ariz. Citizens killed, 2.

September 19 .... Foster Springs, Indian Territory. Detachment of Tr. B, 10th U. S. Cav. Capt. J. B. Van de Wiele in command. Soldiers killed, 1. Indians killed, 2. Indians wounded, 3.

September 22 .... Ft. Sill, Indian Territory. Citizens killed, 2. Indians killed 2 herders and ran off about 15 head of stock.

October 11 .... Freshwater fork of Brazos River, Texas. Trs. A, F, G, H, and K, 4th U. S. Cav. Col. R. S. Mackenzie in command. Soldiers killed, 1.

October 14 .... Cienega Sauz, Ariz. Citizens killed, 1. Citizens wounded, 1.

October 19 .... Freshwater fork of Brazos River, Texas. Trs. A, F, G, H, and K, 4th U. S. Cav. Col. R. S. Mackenzie in command. Col. Mackenzie wounded. Indians killed, 2.

October 24 .... Horseshoe Canon, Ariz. Tr. K, 3rd U. S. Cav. Capt. Gerald Russell in command. Citizens killed, 1. Soldiers wounded, 1.

November 5 .... Near Wickenburgh, Ariz. Attack on mail stage. Citizens killed, 6. Citizens wounded, 2.

1872

January 20 .... Between Tucson and Camp Bowie, Ariz. Attack on stage. Citizens killed, 3. Citizens wounded, 1.

February 9 .... North Concho River, Texas. Detachment of Tr. B, 4th U. S. Cav. Capt. Joseph Rendlebrock in command.

February 22 .... Cullumber's Station Ariz. Citizens killed, 2.

February 26 .... Camp Bowie, Ariz. Citizens killed, 1. Citizens wounded, 1.

March 17 .... Camp Verde, Ariz. Citizens killed, 1.

March 27—28 .... Near Ft. Concho, Texas. Detachment of Tr. I, 4th U. S. Cav. Sergt. Wm. Wilson in command. Indians killed, 2. Indians wounded, 3. Indians captured, 1.

April 17 .... Near Camp Apache, Ariz. Detachment of Co. D, 21st U. S. Infty. Soldiers killed, 1.

April 17 .... Mint Valley, Ariz. Citizens killed, 1.

April 20 .... Near Howard's Well, Texas. Trs. A and H, 9th U. S. Cav. Capt. Michael Cooney in command. Lieut. F. R. Vincent mortally wounded. Indians killed, 6.

April 20 .... Near Wormser, Ariz. Citizens killed, 2.

April 21 .... Texas. Tr. C, 4th U. S. Cav. Capt. J. A. Wilcox in command. Lost 14 horses and 2 mules.

April 25 .... Tierra Amarilla, N. M. Detachment of Tr. K, 8th U. S. Cav. Non-commissioned officer in command. Indians killed, 3.

April 25 .... Juniper Mountains, Ariz. Detachment of Tr. K, 5th U. S. Cav.

April 26 .... South Fork of Loupe River, Nebr. Tr. B, 3rd U. S. Cav. Capt. Chas. Meinhold in command. Indians killed, 3.

April 26 .... Near Camp Crittenden, Ariz. Citizens killed, 1.

April 27 .... Sonoita Valley, Ariz. Citizens killed, 2. Citizens wounded, 1.

May 2 .... Near La Bonte Creek, Wyo. Detachments of Cos. D, E, F, and G, 14th U. S. Infty. Mail escort. Sergt. J. A. Mularky in command. Soldiers killed, 1.

May 4 .... Between Tucson and Camp Bowie, Ariz. Mail. Soldiers killed, 1.

May 5 .... Scout from Camp Hualpai, Ariz. Detachment of Tr. K, 5th U. S. Cav. Sergt. R. Stauffer in command. Indians killed, 5. Indians wounded, 12.

May 6 .... Tierra Amarilla, N. M. Detachments of Trs. E and K, 8th U. S. Cav. Lieut. J. D. Stevenson in command. Soldiers killed, 1. Soldiers wounded, 1. Indians killed, 1. Indians wounded, 1. Troops attacked by a band of Ute Indians.

May 10 .... Near Camp Verde, Ariz. Citizens killed, 3.

May 12 .... Between Big and Little Washita River, Texas. Detachment of Tr. C, 4th U. S. Cav. Capt. J. A. Wilcox in command. Soldiers wounded, 1. Indians killed, 2. Troops attacked by the Kiowas.

May 19 .... Scout from Camp Hualpai, Ariz. Detachment of Tr. K, 5th U. S. Cav. Sergt. R. Stauffer in command. Soldiers wounded, 2. Indians killed, 4.

May 19 .... 25 miles from Ft. Belknap, Texas. Citizens killed, 1. Indians killed, 2. Indians wounded, 2. Attacked by Kiowas.

May 20 .... On the La Pendencia, Texas. Detachment of Tr. C, 9th U. S. Cav.; detachment of Co. K, 24th U. S. Infty.; Indian Scouts. Lieut. Gustavus Valois in command. Troops attacked band of Kickapoos.

May 22 .... Near Prescott, Ariz. Citizens killed, 1.

May 22 .... Between Ft. Dodge, Kans., and Fort Supply, Indian Territory. Detachment of Tr. E, 6th U. S. Cav. Acting as couriers. Soldiers killed, 1. Soldiers wounded, 1.

May 22 .... Sonoita Valley, Ariz. Citizens killed, 1.

May 23 .... Sycamore Canyon, Ariz. Detachment of Tr. A, 1st U. S. Cav. Lieut. W. H. Boyle, 21st U. S. Infty., in command.

May 24 .... On Lost Creek, Texas. Detachment of 4th U. S. Cav. Capt. E. M. Heyl in command. Attacked by Comanches. Soldiers killed, 1. One horse killed.

June 10 .... Bill Williams' Mountain, Ariz. Detachment of Tr. A, 1st U. S. Cav. Lieut. Thos. Garvey in command. Soldiers killed, 1. Soldiers wounded, 1.

June 11 .... Vicinity of Whipple Barracks, Ariz. Detachment of Tr. A, 1st U. S. Cav. Fight with Apache Indians.

June 13 .... Near Prescott, Ariz. Citizens killed, 1.

June 14 .... Ponca Agency, Dak. Detachments of Cos, B, D, G, H, and K, 22nd U. S. Infty. Lieut. O. M. Smith in command.

June 15 .... Granite Mountains, Ariz. Citizens wounded, 2.

June 15 .... Johnson's Station, Texas. Detachment of Co. H, 11th U. S. Infty. Corporal Hickey in command. Indians killed, 2.

July 1 .... Gardiner's Ranch, Sonora Valley, Ariz. Detachment of Tr. F, 5th U. S. Cav.

July 12 .... Deep River, Indian Territory. Trs. A and L, 10th U. S. Cav. Capt. Nicholas Nolan in command.

July 13 .... Canon of Whetstone Mountains, Ariz. Detachment of Tr. F, 5th U. S. Cav. Lieut. W. P. Hall in command. Soldiers wounded, 2. Indians killed, 4.

July 22 .... Otter Creek, Indian Territory. Trs. A and L, 10th U. S. Cav. Capt. Nicholas Nolan in command. Indians wounded, 1.

July 25 .... Moore's ranch, Sonora Valley, Ariz. Detachment of Tr. F, 5th U. S. Cav.

July 27 .... Mount Graham, Ariz. Tr. A, 8th U. S. Cav. Lieut. Wm. Stephenson in command. Indians killed, 1.

July 28 .... Central Station, Texas. Detachment of Co. K, 25th U. S. Infty. Sergt. J. Walker in command.

July 26 to October 15 .... First Yellowstone expedition. Cos. A, B, C, F, H, and K, 8th U. S. Infty.; Cos. A, C, and F, 17th U. S. Infty.; Cos. D, F, and G, 22nd U. S. Infty.; and Indian Scouts. Col. D. S. Stanley, 22nd U. S. Infty., in command. Lieut. Eben Crosby, 17th U. S. Infty., killed October 3, 1872,; and Lieut. L. D. Adair, mortally wounded, same day, while out hunting. Citizens killed, 1.

August 6 .... Chiricahua Mountains, Ariz. Tr. A, 8th U. S. Cav. Lieut. Wm. Stephenson in command. Indians killed, 2.

August 14 .... Near Prior's Fork, Mont. Trs. F, G, H, and L, 2nd U. S. Cav.; Cos. C, E, G, and I, 7th U. S. Infty. Major E. M. Baker, 2nd U. S. Cav., in command. Soldiers killed, 1. Citizens killed, 1. Soldiers wounded, 5. Indians killed, 2. Indians wounded, 10. Attacked by Sioux and Cheyennes.

August 15 .... Palo Duro Creek, N. M. Tr. B, 8th U. S. Cav. Capt. Wm. McCleave in command. Soldiers wounded, 1. Indians killed, 4. Indians wounded, 8.

August 16 .... Near Yellowstone River, Mont. Expedition commanded by Col. D. S. Stanley, 22nd U. S. Infty., was attacked by
a large body of Indians.
August 17 .... On the Yellowstone River, Mont. Capt. L. Thompson
commanding expedition. One man of Tr. L, 2nd U. S. Cav.
was reported wounded.
August 18 .... At mouth of Powder River, Mont. Cos. D, F, and G,
22nd U. S. Infty. Col. D. S. Stanley commanding.
August 21—22 .... On O'Fallon's Creek, Mont. Cos. D, F, and G,
22nd U. S. Infty. Col. D. S. Stanley commanding.
August 26 .... Near Ft. McKeen, Dak. Detachments of Cos. B, and
C, 6th U. S. Infty.; Indian scouts. Soldiers killed, 6. Citi-
zens killed, 2. Attacked by 125 Sioux.
August 27 .... Davidson's Canon, Ariz. Detachment of Tr. F, 5th
U. S. Cav. Lieut. R. T. Stewart in command. Lieut. Stewart
killed. Soldiers killed, 1. Citizens killed, 2.
September 4 .... Near Camp Mojave, Ariz. Citizens killed, 1.
September 8 .... Camp Date Creek, Ariz. Tr. E, 5th U. S. Cav.
September 10—13 .... Between Beaver Creek and Sweet Water,
Wyo. Tr. B, 2nd U. S. Cav. Lieut. Randolph Norwood in
command. Indians wounded, 1.
September 19 .... Jones County, Texas. Detachment of one sergeant
and seven men, 4th U. S. Cav., and two Tonkawa scouts. At-
tacked about 50 Comanche Indians. One Mexican chief killed.
Recaptured 11 stolen horses.
September 25 .... Muchos Canon, Santa Maria River, Ariz. Trs. B,
C, and K, 5th U. S. Cav. Capt. J. W. Mason in command.
Indians killed, 40.
September 29 .... North Fork of Red River, Texas. Trs. A, D, F, I,
and L, 4th U. S. Cav.; and Detachment of Ton-Ka-Wa
Scouts. Col. R. S. Mackenzie in command. Soldiers killed,
1. Soldiers wounded, 3. Indians killed, 23. Indians wound-
ed, 1. Indians captured, 120. Troops attacked village of
200 lodges.
September 30 .... Squaw Peak, Ariz. Detachment of Tr. A, 1st U.
S. Cav. Lieut. Max Wesendorff in command. Indians killed,
17. Indians captured, 1.
September 30 .... Near Camp Crittenden, Ariz. Tr. F, 5th U. S. Cav.
Sergt. Geo. Stewart in command. Soldiers killed, 4.
October 2 .... Ft. McKeen, Dak. Co. C, 6th U. S. Infty., and Indian
Scouts. Lieut. Col. Daniel Huston, Jr., in command. Soldiers
killed, 3. Soldiers wounded, 1. About 300 Sioux attacked the
fort.
October 3 .... Jones County, Texas. Detachment of Tonkawa scouts
made an attack on a camp of Comanches. No details given.
October 14 .... Ft. McKeen, Dak. Co. C, 6th U. S. Infty.; Co. H. 17th
U. S. Infty.; and Indian Scouts. Lieut. Col. W. P. Carlin,
17th U. S. Infty., in command. Citizens killed, 2. Indians
killed, 3.
October 25—November 3 .... Santa Maria Mountains, or Sycamore
Creek, Ariz. Trs. B, C, and K, 5th U. S. Cav. Capt. J. W.
Mason in command. Indians killed, 9.

November 3 .... Attack on Ft. McKeen, Dak. Cos. B, and C, 6th U. S. Infty.; Co. H, 17th U. S. Infty.; and Indian Scouts.

November 25 .... Red Rocks or Hell Canyon, Ariz. Tr. C, 5th U. S. Cav.; and Piute Scouts. Capt. Emil Adam in command. Soldiers killed, 1. Indians killed, 11. Indians captured, 4.

November 26 .... Red Rock Country, Ariz. Tr. B, 5th U. S. Cav.

November 29 .... Near Lost River, Ore. Detachment of Tr. B, 1st U. S. Cav. Capt. James Jackson in command. Soldiers killed, 1. Soldiers wounded, 7. Indians killed, 8. Fight with Captain Jack's band of Modoc Indians.

November 29, 1872 to June 1, 1873 .... Modoc campaign. Gen. E. R. S. Canby, Col. A. C. Gillem, and Col. J. C. Davis in command.

December 2 .... Land's Ranch or Tule Lake, Calif. Tr. G, 1st U. S. Cav. Capt. R. F. Bernard in command. Soldiers killed, 1. Soldiers wounded, 1.

December 6 .... Near the Rio Grande, Texas. Sergeant Bruce and six men, 9th U. S. Cav., attacked a band of Mexican cattle thieves and recaptured 59 head of stolen cattle.

December 7—8 .... Red Rock Country, Ariz. Detachments of Tr. K, 5th U. S. Cav., and Co. G, 23rd U. S. Infty.; and Indian Scouts. Lieut. Frank Michler, 5th U. S. Cav., in command. Indians killed, 12.

December 11 .... Bad Rock Mountain, north of old Ft. Reno, Ariz. Detachments of Trs. L and M, 1st U. S. Cav.; Detachment of Co. I, 23rd U. S. Infty.; and Indian Scouts. Lieut. Thos. Garvey, 1st U. S. Cav., in command. Indians killed, 14.

December 13 .... Mazatzal Mountains, north of old Fort Reno, Ariz. Detachments of Trs. L and M, 1st U. S. Cav.; Detachment of Co. I, 23rd U. S. Infty.; and Indian Scouts. Lieut W. C. Manning, 23rd U. S. Infty.; in command. Indians killed, 11. Indians captured, 6. Fight with Tonto-Apache Indians.

December 14 .... Indian Run, Ariz. Tr. E, 5th U. S. Cav. Capt. G. F. Price in command. Indians captured, 9.

December 21 .... At Land's Ranch, Tule Lake, Calif. Tr. G, 1st U. S. Cav. Capt. R. F. Bernard in command. Pvt. Sydney A. Smith killed. Pvt. William Donahue fatally wounded. Attack by Modoc Indians on wagon train from an ambuscade about one mile from Capt. Bernard's Camp.

December 28 .... Salt River Canon, Ariz. Tr. G, L and M, 5th U. S. Cav.; and Indian Scouts. Capt. W. H. Brown in command. Soldiers killed, 1. Soldiers wounded, 1. Indians killed, 57. Indians captured, 20.

December 28 .... Red Rock Springs and Red Rock Valley, Ariz. Detachment of Tr. H, 5th U. S. Cav.

December 30 .... Mouth of Baby Canon, Ariz. Detachment of Tr E, 5th U. S. Cav. Sergt. W. L. Day in command. Indians killed, 6. Indians wounded, 1. Indians captured, 2.

1873

January 2 .... Clear Creek Canon, Ariz. Detachment of Tr. K, 5th U. S. Cav.; Co. G, 23rd U. S. Infty.; and Indian Scouts. Lieut.

W. F. Rice, 23rd U. S. Infty., in command. Soldiers wounded, 1.

January 12 .... Tule Lake, Calif. Tr. G, 1st U. S. Cav., Capt. R. F. Bernard in command. Soldiers wounded, 1.

January 16 .... Superstition Mountain, Ariz. Trs. B, C, G, H, L, and M, 5th U. S. Cav. Capt. W. H. Brown in command. Indians killed, 4. Indians captured, 12.

January 16 .... In Lava Beds, Tule Lake, Calif. Trs. B, F, G, and Detachment of Tr. H, 1st U. S. Cav. Capt. R. F. Bernard in command. A preliminary skirmish as troops were getting into position for attack of January 17.

January 17 .... Modoc Caves in Lava Beds, near Tule Lake, Calif. Trs. B, F, and G, 1st U. S. Cav.; Cos. B, C. and Detachment of Co. F, 21st U. S. Infty.; and California and Oregon Vols. Lieut. Col. Frank Wheaton, 21st U. S. Infty., in command. Soldiers killed, 9. Lieuts. David Perry and J. M. Kyle, 1st U. S. Cav., and Lieut. G. W. Roberts, Calif. Vols., wounded. Soldiers wounded, 27.

January 19 .... East fork of Verde River, Ariz. Detachment of Scouts from Tr. E, 5th U. S. Cav. Sergt. W. L. Day in command. Indians killed, 5.

January 20 .... Lower Mimbres, N. M. Tr. I, 8th U. S. Cav. Lieut. J. D. Stevenson in command. Indians killed, 1.

January 22 .... Tonto Creek, Ariz. Tr. K, 5th U. S. Cav. Lieut. Frank Michler in command. Soldiers killed, 1. Indians killed, 17.

January 22 .... Between Tule Lake and Applegate's Ranch, Calif. Tr. G, 1st U. S. Cav. Capt. R. F. Bernard in command. Indians killed, 1.

February 2 .... Near Ft. Whipple, Ariz. Detachment of Tr. A, 1st U. S. Cav. Skirmish with Apache Indians.

February 6 .... Hell Canon, Ariz. Detachment of Tr. A, 1st U. S. Cav. Capt. Thos. McGregor in command. Indians killed, 2. Indians captured, 1.

February 13 .... Near Ft. Whipple, Ariz. Detachment of Tr. A, 1st U. S. Cav. Skirmish with Apache Indians.

February 20 .... Near Fossil Creek, Ariz. Tr. I, 1st U. S. Cav. Capt. C. C. C. Carr in command. Indians killed, 5. Indians captured, 4.

February 26 .... Angostura, N. M. Tr. L, 8th U. S. Cav. Sergt. J. F. Rowalt in command. Indians killed, 5. Indians wounded, 7.

March 19 .... Mazatzal Mountains, Ariz. Tr. K, 5th U. S. Cav. Lieut. Frank Michler in command. Indians killed, 8. Indians captured, 5.

March 25 .... Near Turret Mountains, Ariz. Detachment of Tr. A, 5th U. S. Cav. Sergt. S. M. Hill in command. Indians killed, 10. Indians captured, 3.

March 27 .... Turret Mountains, Ariz. Detachment of Tr. A, 5th U. S. Cav.; Detachment of Co. I, 23rd U. S. Infty.; and Indian Scouts. Capt. G. M. Randall, 23rd U. S. Infty., in command. Indians killed, 23. Indians captured, 10.

April 11—20 .... Lava Beds, Calif. Trs. B, F, G, H. and K, 1st U. S. Cav.; Cos. E, and G, 12th U. S. Infty.; Cos. B, C, and I, 21st

U. S. Infty.; and Bat. A, B, E, G, H, and K, 4th U. S. Artillery; and Indian scouts. Brig. Gen. E. R. S. Canby and Col. A. C. Gillem, 1st U. S. Cav., in command. Gen. E. R. S. Canby killed. Soldiers killed, 6. Citizens killed, 1. Lieut. Walter Sherwood, 21st U. S. Infty., wounded April 11; and Lieut. C. P. Eagen, 12th U. S. Infty., wounded April 15. Soldiers wounded, 13. Citizens wounded, 2.

April 22 .... Diamond Butte, Ariz. Detachment of Trs. L and M, 1st U. S. Cav.; Detachment of Co. I, 23rd U. S. Infty., and Indian Scouts.

April 25 .... Near Canon Creek, Ariz. Detachments of Trs. L, and M, 1st U. S. Cav.; Detachment of Co. I, 23rd U. S. Infty., and Indian Scouts. Capt. G. M. Randall, 23rd U. S. Infty., in command. Surrender of Del Chay and his band.

April 26 .... Lava Beds, Calif. Bat. A and K, 4th U. S. Artillery; Co. E, 12th U. S. Infty. Capt. Evan Thomas, 4th U. S. Artillery, in command. Capt. Evan Thomas and Lieuts. Albion Howe, Arthur Cranston, 4th Art., and T. F. Wright, 12th U. S. Infty., killed. Soldiers killed, 18. Lieut. G. M. Harris, 4th Art., wounded. Acting Asst. Surgeon B. G. Semig wounded. Soldiers wounded, 16. Citizens wounded, 1.

April 27 .... Eagle Springs, Texas. Detachment of Co. B, 25th U. S. Infty. Corp. E. Parker in command.

April 30 .... Near Ft. Sill, Ind. Ter. Eleven men of the Tenth U. S. Cav. Lieut. Wm. R. Harmon in command. Attacked a band of thieves and recaptured 36 horses.

May .... Barrilla Springs, Texas. Detachment of Co. D, 25th U. S. Infty. Sergt. W. Smith in command.

May 6 .... Santa Maria River, Ariz. Tr. A, 1st U. S. Cav. Capt. Thos. McGregor in command. Indians killed, 4.

May 7 .... Lava Beds, Calif. Co. B, C, I, and Detachment of Co. F, 21st U. S. Infty. Major E. C. Mason, in command. Soldiers wounded, 2.

May 7 .... Lava Beds, Calif. Trs. B, and G, 1st U. S. Cav.; Bat. B, 4th U. S. Artillery. Capt. H. C. Hasbrouck, 4th U. S. Art., in command. Soldiers wounded, 1.

May 7 .... Fort A. Lincoln, Dak. Cos. B and C, 6th U. S. Infty., Co. H, 7th U. S. Infty.; and Indian Scouts. Lieut. Col. W. P. Carlin, 17th U. S. Infty., in command. Indians killed, 1. Indians wounded, 3. About 100 Sioux attacked the Post.

May 10 .... Lake Soras, Calif. Trs. B and G, 1st U. S. Cav.; Bat. B, 4th U. S. Art.; Indian Scouts. Capt. H. C. Hasbrouck, 4th U. S. Art., in command. Soldiers killed, 2. Soldiers wounded, 7. Indians killed, 1. Indians wounded, 2.

May 17 .... Near Butte Creek, Ore. Trs. B and G. 1st U. S. Cav.; Bat. B, 4th U. S. Art.; Indian Scouts. Capt. H. C. Hasbrouck, 4th U. S. Art., in command. Indians killed, 2.

May 18 .... Near Remolina, Mexico. Trs. A, B, C, E, I, and M, 4th U. S. Cav.; and Indian Scouts. Col. R. S. Mackenzie, 4th U. S. Cav., in command. Soldiers wounded, 3. Indians killed, 19. Indians wounded, 2. Indians captured, 42. Troops attacked and destroyed a village of 50 or 60 lodges of Kickapoos and Lipan Indians. The column marched at a trot or a gallop, a distance of 75 miles, between 1 o'clock in the afternoon of the previous day and 6 o'clock in the morning of the day of the attack, in order to reach and surprise this village whose location had been reported. The pack train of supplies was dropped during this rapid march, and for two days the troops were without other rations than a few crackers carried in their pockets. Among the prisoners taken was Costilietos, the principal chief of the Lipans.

May 19 .... Opposite Fairchild's Ranch, near Lava Beds, Calif. Tr. B, 1st U. S. Cav. Fight with Modoc Indians.

May 22 .... Near Fairchild's Ranch, Calif. Col. J. C. Davis in command. Indians captured, 150. Surrender of part of the Modoc Indians.

May 27 .... San Carlos Agency, Ariz. Lieut. Jacob Almy murdered by Indians.

May 29 .... Tularosa River, N. M. Detachment of Tr. D, 8th U. S. Cav.

May 30 .... Langell's Valley, Calif. Trs. B and G, 1st U. S. Cav.; Bat. B, 4th U. S. Art.; and Indian Scouts. Major John Green, 1st U. S. Cav., in command. Indians captured, 33. Capture of Scar-face Charley, Chonchin, and Boston Charley, Modoc Indians.

June 1 .... Willow Creek, Calif. Tr. F, 1st U. S. Cav. Capt. David Perry in command. Indians captured, 7. Capture of Captain Jack.

June 15-17 ——— Ft. A. Lincoln, Dak. Co. H, 17th U. S. Infty.; and Cos. B and C, 6th U. S. Infty. Lieut. Col. W. P. Carlin, 17th U. S. Infty,. in command. Soldiers killed, 1. Indians killed, 4. Indians wounded, 8.

June 16 .... Forks of Tonto Creek, Ariz. Detachment of Tr. C, 5th U. S. Cav.; Indian Scouts. Lieut. J. B. Babcock in command. Soldiers wounded, 1. Indians killed, 14. Indians captured, 5.

July 12 .... Live Oak Creek, Ind. Ter. Tr. L, 4th U. S. Cav. Capt. T. J. Wint in command.

July 13 .... Canada Alamosa, N. M. Tr. C, 8th U. S. Cav. Capt. G. W. Chilson in command. Soldiers killed, 1. Indians killed, 3. 12 horses and one mule stolen by the Indians were recaptured.

July 14 .... Lipan Creek, Texas. Tr. L, 4th U. S. Cav., Capt. T. J. Wint in command.

August 4 .... Tongue River, Mont. Trs. A and B, 7th U. S. Cav. Capt. Myles Moylan in command. Soldiers wounded, 1. Indians wounded, 1. Stanley's Yellowstone Expedition.

August 4 .... On the Yellowstone River, Mont. Trs. A, B, E, F. G, K, L, and M, 7th U. S. Cav.; and Indian Scouts. Lieut. Col. G. A. Custer in command. Troops were attacked by several hundred Sioux. Lieut. C. Braden wounded. Soldiers killed, 4. Soldiers wounded, 3.

August 11 .... On the Yellowstone River, Mont. Trs. A, B, E, F, G, K, L and M, 7th U. S. Cav.; and Indian Scouts. Lieut. Col. G. A. Custer in command. Again attacked by a large body of Sioux. Indians killed, 4. Indians wounded, 12 .

August 19 .... Barrilla Springs, Texas. Detachment of Co. E, 25th
U. S. Infty. Corpl. G. Collins in command. Indians killed,
1.
August 31 .... Near Pease River, Texas. Trs. E, and I, 10th U. S.
Cav. Capt. T. A. Baldwin in command. Indians wounded,
1.
September .... Sierra San Mater, N. M. Tr. H, 8th U. S. Cav. Lieut.
H. J. Farnsworth in command. Indians killed, 2.
September 18 .... North Laramie River. Trs. K and E, 2nd U. S. Cav.
Capt. J. Egan in command. Captured 18 horses and mules.
September 20 .... Near Ft. Fetterman, Wyo. Tr. K, 2nd U. S. Cav.
Capt. James Egan in command.
September 23 .... Hardscrabble Creek, or Mescal Range, Ariz. De-
tachment of Tr. K, 5th U. S. Cav.; Indian Scouts. Lieut. W.
S. Schuyler in command. Indians killed, 14. Indians captured,
5.
September 29 .... Sierra Ancha, Ariz. Detachment of Trs. F, I, and
L, 5th U. S. Cav.; Detachment of Co. H, 23rd U. S. Infty.;
Indian Scouts. Capt. W. H. Brown, 5th U. S. Cav., in com-
mand. Indians killed, 2. Indians captured, 4.
September 30 .... Mesquite Flats, Texas. Trs. E and I, 10th U. S. Cav.
Capt. T. A. Baldwin in command. Recaptured 9 stolen horses.
October 1 .... Central Station, Texas. Detachment of Co. K, 25th U.
S. Infty. Sergt. B. Mew in command.
October 1 .... Guadaloupe Mountains, N. M. Tr. C, 8th U. S. Cav.
Capt. G. W. Chilson in command. Indians killed, 3. Indians
wounded, 1.
October 1 .... Camp Colorado, Texas. Detachment consisting of a
sergeant and 13 soldiers were attacked by a party of Com-
anches. Indians wounded, 1.
October 8 .... Chiricahua Mountains, Ariz. Tr. A, 8th U. S. Cav.
Capt. A. B. Wells in command.
October 28—30 .... Mazatzal Mountains, Sycamore Springs or Sun-
flower Valley, Ariz. Detachments of Trs. F and L, 5th U.
S. Cav.; Detachment of Co. H, 23rd U. S. Infty.; and Indian
Scouts. Capt. W. H. Brown, 5th U. S. Cav., in command. In-
dians killed, 25. Indians captured, 6.
October 25 .... Little Cabin Creek, Texas. 25 men of the 7th U. S.
Cav. Lieut. J. B. Kerr in command. Captured a party of 8
cattle thieves. 70 horses and 200 head of cattle were recap-
tured.
October 30 .... Pajarit Springs, N. M. Tr. D, 8th U. S. Cav. Lieut.
A. G. Hennisee in command. Indians captured, 18.
November 25 .... Near Ehrenberg, Ariz. Detachment of Tr. G, 5th
U. S. Cav.; Indian Scouts.
December 4 .... East Fork of the Verde River, Ariz. Tr. K, 5th U. S.
Cav.; and Indian Scouts. Lieut. W. S. Schuyler in command.
Indians killed, 15.
December 5 .... Elm Creek, Texas. Detachment of Tr. D, 10th U. S.
Cav. Lieut. E. P. Turner in command. Indians killed, 4. In-
dians captured, 16. Recovered about 1000 head of stolen
cattle.
December 8—January 20, 1874—Scout from San Carlos, Ariz. De-

tachment of Tr. C, 5th U. S. Cav.; Indian Scouts. Lieut. W. F. Rice, 23rd U. S. Infty., in command. Indians killed, 25. Indians captured, 17.

December 9 .... West Fork of the Nueces River, Texas. Tr. B, 4th U. S. Cav. Lieut. C. L. Hudson in command.

December 10 .... Kickapoo Springs, Texas. Detachment of Trs. A, B, C, and I, 4th U. S. Cav.; and Indian Scouts. Lieut. C. L. Hudson in command. Soldiers wounded, 1. Indians killed, 9. Recaptured 81 horses.

December 21 .... Near Ehrenberg, Ariz. Tr. G, 5th U. S. Cav. Capt. James Burns in command. Indians killed, 6. Indians captured, 1.

December 23 .... Cave Creek, Ariz. Tr. K, 5th U. S. Cav.; Indian Scouts. Lieut. W. S. Schuyler in command. Indians killed, 9. Indians wounded, 3.

December 27 .... Deep Red Creek, Ind. Ter. Detachment of the 25th U. S. Infty. Corporal Wright in command. Indians wounded, 1.

December 31 .... Sunflower Valley, near Fort Reno, Ariz. Tr. B, 5th U. S. Cav.; and Scouts. Lieut. J. B. Babcock in command. Indians killed, 7. Indians captured, 11.

December 31 .... Eagle Springs, Texas. Detachment of a sergeant and 3 privates of Co. B, 25th U. S. Infty. attacked by about 15 Indians. Indians wounded, 1.

1874

January 4 .... Wild Rye Creek, Ariz. Tr. B, 5th U. S. Cav.; and Indian Scouts. Lieut. J. B. Babcock in command. Indians killed, 4.

January 8 .... Pleasant Valley, Headwaters of Cherry Creek, Ariz. Tr. B, 5th U. S. Cav.; and Indian Scouts. Lieut. J. B. Babcock in command. Indians killed, 2.

January 10 .... Canon Creek, Ariz. Tr. K, 5th U. S. Cav., and Indian Scouts. Lieut. W. S. Schuyler in command. Indians killed, 4. Indians wounded, 3. Indians captured, 3.

February 2 .... Home Creek, Texas. Detachment of Tr. A, 10th U. S. Cav. Sergt. T. Allsup in command.

February 5 .... Double Mountain, Fork of the Brazos River, Texas. Tr. G, and Detachment of Tr. D, 10th U. S. Cav.; Co. F, and Detachments of Cos. A and G, 11th U. S. Infantry; and Indian Scouts. Lieut. Col. G. P. Buell, 11th U. S. Infty., in command. Soldiers wounded, 1. Indians killed, 10. Captured 65 horses. Troops attacked a Camp of Comanches.

February 9 .... Cottonwood Creek, near Laramie Peak, Wyo. Detachment of 2nd U. S. Cav., and 14th U. S. Infty. Lieut. L. H. Robinson, 14th U. S. Infty., in command. Acting as lumber train guard. Lieut. Robinson killed. Soldiers killed, 1, —Corporal Coleman. This seemed to be the signal for trouble at Red Cloud's and Spotted Tail's Agencies. Troops sent to protect these agencies, hostile bands forced to withdraw. The hostiles aroused the Northern Cheyennes and Arapahoes who were in the valley of the Big Horn, where the Wind River breaks through the Big Horn range of mountains.

From here they commenced a series of raids on the Shoshones and settlers in the valleys of the Big and Little Popoagie Rivers.

February 20 to April 21 .... Scout in Bill Williams' Mountains, Ariz. Detachment of Tr. G, 5th U. S. Cav. Lieut. E. D. Thomas in command. Indians killed, 3.

March 8 .... Pinal Mountains, Ariz. Detachments of Trs. B, F, H, I, L, and M, 5th U. S. Cav.; and Indian Scouts. Capt. G. M. Randall, 23rd U. S. Infty., in command. Indians killed, 12. Indians captured, 25.

March 15 .... Pinal Mountains, Ariz. Tr. H, and Detachments of Trs. F and M, 5th U. S. Cav. Capt. J. M. Hamilton in command. Soldiers wounded, 2.

March 25—26 .... Superstition Mountains, Ariz. Tr. K, 5th U. S. Cav. Lieut. W. S. Schuyler in command. Indians killed, 12. Indians captured, 2.

April .... China Tree Creek, Texas. Tr. K, 10th U. S. Cav.; Detachment of Co. C, 25th U. S. Infty.; Co. D, 11th U. S. Infty. Capt. W. C. Beach, 11th U. S. Infty., in command. Indians wounded, 1.

April 2 .... Pinal Creek, Ariz. Trs. F, L, and M, 5th U. S. Cav.; and Indian Scouts. Lieut. A. B. Bache in command. Indians killed, 31. Indians captured, 50.

April 3—14 .... Pinal Mountains, Ariz. Trs. B, H, and I, 5th U. S. Cav.; and Indian Scouts. Capt. J. M. Hamilton in command. Indians killed, 14. Indians captured, 28.

April 4 .... Grand Canon of the Colorado, (near), Ariz. Detachment of Tr. G, 5th U. S. Cav.

April 11 .... Bull Bear Creek, Ind. Ter. Detachment of Tr. G, 6th U. S. Cav. Capt. T. C. Tupper in command.

April 23 .... Near Ft. A. Lincoln, Dak. Trs. A, B, E, F, G, and L, 7th U. S. Cav. Lieut. Col. G. A. Custer in command. Indians wounded, 1.

April 28 .... Arivaypa Mountains, Ariz. Tr. K, 5th U. S. Cav. Lieut. W. S. Schuyler in command. Indians killed, 23. Indians captured, 12.

May 2 .... Between the Red River and Big Wishita, Texas. Detachment of Tr. K, 10th U. S. Cav. Lieut. Q. O'M. Gillmore in command. No casualties.

May 9 .... Tonto Creek, Ariz. Detachment of Tr. K, 5th U. S. Cav.; and Indian Scouts. Lieut. C. H. Heyl, 23rd U. S. Infty., in command. Indians killed, 3. Indians captured, 2.

May 17—18 .... Four Peaks, Mazatzal Mountains, Ariz. Detachments of Trs. E, and K, 5th U. S. Cav. Lieut. W. S. Schuyler in command. Indians killed, 38. Indians captured, 12.

May 18 .... Carrizo Mountains, Texas. Detachment of Co. B, 25th U. S. Infty. Capt. Charles Bentzoni in command. No casualties.

May 21 to June 6 .... Near Diamond Butte, Ariz. Detachment of Tr. K, 5th U. S. Cav. Lieut. Charles King in command. Indians killed, 19. Diamond Butte expedition, including Black Mesa.

May 27 .... Sierra Anchas, Ariz. Detachment of Tr. A, 5th U. S.

Cav.; and Indian Scouts. Lieut. C. H. Heyl, 23rd U. S. Infty., in command. Soldiers wounded, 1. Indians killed, 4. Indians captured, 9.

June 5 ...... Sierra Anchas, Ariz. Detachment of Tr. I, 5th U. S. Cav.

June 8 ...... Pleasant Valley, Ariz. Tr. B, 5th U. S. Cav.; and Indian Scouts. Lieut. J. B. Babcock in command. Indians killed, 2.

June 19 ...... Buffalo Creek, Ind. Ter. Detachment of Tr. K, 6th U. S. Cav.; and Detachment of Co. D, 3rd U. S. Infty. Mail Escort. Soldiers wounded, 1.

June 21 ...... Buffalo Creek, Ind. Ter. Detachment of Tr. G, 6th U. S. Cav.; and Co. A, 3rd U. S. Infty. Maj. C. E. Compton, 6th U. S. Cav., in command. On mail escort. Soldiers wounded, 1. Citizens wounded, 1. Indians wounded, 2.

June 24 ...... Bear Creek Redoubt, Kans. Detachment of Tr. G, 6th U. S. Cav.; and Co. A, 3rd U. S. Infty. Maj. C. E. Compton, 6th U. S. Cav., in command. Indians killed, 6. Indians wounded, 11.

July 2 ...... Castle Dome Mountains, Ariz. Tr. G, 5th U. S. Cav.

July 4 ...... Near Bad Water Branch of Wind River or Snake Mountains or Owl Mountains, Wyo. Tr. B, 2nd U. S. Cav.; and Indian Scouts. Capt. A. E. Bates in command. Soldiers killed, 4. Lieut. R. H. Young, 4th U. S. Infty., wounded. Soldiers wounded, 5. Indians killed, 26. Indians wounded, 20. Indians retired to Pumpkin Butte and sent word to Ft. Fetterman asking if the troops wanted war. The reply was "Yes," and that they would fight until the Indians stopped their depredations and came to the agency, which most of them did at once. Small parties of Sioux remained out and continued plundering and killing until they were driven away.

July 8—13 ...... Crow Agency, Mont. Detachment of Co. A, 7th U. S. Infty. Sergt. J. Mason in command.

July 13 ...... 30 miles west of Camp Date Creek, Ariz. Tr. G, 5th U. S. Cav.

July 13 ...... Near the Sweetwater, Wyo. Tr. B, 2nd U. S.Cav. Capt. A. E. Bates in command. Indians killed, 1. Horses captured, 7.

July 19 ...... Rattlesnake Hills, Wyo. Tr. B, 2nd U. S. Cav.; and Indian Scouts. Capt. A. E. Bates in command. Soldiers wounded, 1. Indians killed, 1.

July 20 ...... Polo Pinto County, Texas. Detachment of 2 officers, 9 men, and 9 Tonkawa scouts. Lieut. Col. G. P. Buell, 11th U. S. Infty., in command. Horses captured, 1.

August 15 ...... Near San Carlos, Ariz. Indian Scouts under Chief Desaline. Indians killed, 9. Indians captured, 119.

August 18 ...... Black Mesa, Ariz. Indian Scouts. Guide C. E. Cooley in command. Indians killed, 13.

August 19 ...... Adobe Walls, Texas. Detachment of 6th U. S. Cav.; and White and Indian Scouts. Lieut. F. D. Baldwin, 5th U. S. Infty., in command. Defeated and repulsed an attack by 150 hostile Indians. One Civilian Buffalo Hunter, Geo. Huffman, killed.

August 20 ...... Chicken Creek, now Walnut Creek, Texas. Detachment of 6th U. S. Cav.; and White and Indian Scouts. Lieut.

F. D. Baldwin, 5th U. S. Infty., in command. Indians killed, 1. Indians wounded, 1.

August 22 .... North end Sierra Ancha, Ariz. Indian Scouts. Guide C. E. Cooley in command. Indians killed, 10.

August 22—23 .... Wichita Agency, Ind. Ter. Trs. E, H, and L, 10th U. S. Cav.; Co. I, 25th U. S. Infty. Lieut. Col. J. W. Davidson, 10th U. S. Cav., in command. Soldiers wounded, 4. Indians killed, 16. Fight was with the Comanches and Kiowas who attempted to burn out the agency and the Camp of the friendly Indians.

August 30 .... Mulberry Creek or Salt Fork of Red River, Texas. Trs. A, D, F, G, H, I, L, and M, 6th U. S. Cav.; Cos., C, D, E, and I, 5th U. S. Infty. Col. N. A. Miles, 5th U. S. Infty., in command. Soldiers wounded, 1. Indians killed, 3. Citizens wounded, 1.

September 8 .... Elm Fork of Red River, Texas. 3 White Scouts— Lem T. Wilson, W. F. Schmalsle, and Ira Wing. Lieut. F. D. Baldwin, 5th U. S. Infty., in command. This was when Baldwin was carrying despatches from Gen. Miles Camp on Mulberry Creek to Camp Supply, Ind. Ter. These men held off 125 Indians for one whole day. Soldiers wounded, 1. Indians killed, 10.

September 8 .... Wichita River, Texas. Indian Scouts.

September 9 .... Dry Fork of Wichita River, Texas. Co. I, 5th U. S. Infty.; Detachments of Trs. H and I, 6th U. S. Cav.; escort of Col. N. A. Miles supply train. Capt. Wyllys Lyman, 5th U. S. Infty., in command. Lieut. Granville Lewis, 5th U. S. Infty., wounded. Soldiers killed, 1. Citizens wounded, 3. Soldiers wounded, 1.

September 9 .... Sweetwater Creek, Texas. Detachment of Tr. H, 6th U. S. Cav. (Courier of Miles' command). Soldiers wounded, 1.

September 9—12 .... Near Canadian River, Texas. Detachment of Tr. I, 6th U. S. Cav.

September 11—12 .... Near Wichita River, Texas. Detachment of Tr. H, 6th U. S. Cav. (Couriers) Corpl. E. C. Sharpless in command. Soldiers wounded, 4. A detachment of 2 scouts and 4 soldiers from Colonel Miles' command, in endeavoring to communicate with that of Major Price, were attacked by Indians and four of the six wounded, one of the wounded dying in a hole in which the party desperately defended themselves for two days until relieved by troops in that vicinity.

September 11—12 .... McClellan Creek near Wichita River, Texas. Detachment of Tr. M, 6th U. S. Cav. Col. N. A. Miles, 5th U. S. Infty., in command. Soldiers killed, 2. Soldiers wounded, 2.

September 12 .... Between Sweetwater and Dry Fork of Wichita, Texas. Trs. C, K, and L, 8th U. S. Cav. Maj. W. R. Price in command. Indians killed, 2. Indians wounded, 6. Miles' Expedition. Troops had 14 horses killed and wounded. 20 Indian ponies captured.

September 12 .... Near Gageby Creek, Hemphill Co., Texas. The Buffalo Wallow Fight. Detachment of 4 enlisted men of

6th U. S. Cav., and 2 white scouts. Sergt. S. T. Woodhall, Tr. I, 6th Cav., commanding. Attacked by 100 Indians. Soldiers killed, 2. Soldiers wounded, 1. Indians killed, 12.

September 17 .... Headwaters of Cave Creek, Ariz. Detachment of Tr. K, 5th U. S. Cav.; and Indian Scouts. Sergt. A. Garner in command. Soldiers killed, 1. Soldiers wounded, 2. Indians killed, 14. Indians captured, 2.

September 26—28 .... On Red River, near Tule and Palo Duro canyons, Texas. Trs. A, D, E, F, H, I, and K, 4th U. S. Cav. Col. R. S. Mackenzie in command. Soldiers wounded, 1. Indians killed, 4. Surprised five camps of Southern Cheyennes and their allies in a canon, destroyed over 100 lodges and captured their entire outfit, including over 1400 horses and mules.

October .... Near Canadian River, Texas. Trs. E and K, 9th U. S. Cav. Capt. A. E. Hooker in command. Indians killed, 1.

October 4—31 .... Near Ft. Sill, Ind. Ter. Tr. K, 9th U. S. Cav. Capt. Chas. Parker in command. Indians killed, 1.

October 9 .... Salt Fork or Red River, Texas. Co. A, E, F, H, and I, 11th U. S. Infty.; Indian scouts. Lieut. Col. G. P. Buell in command. Troops ran into band of Kiowas, destroyed their Camp, and several hundred lodges. Indians escaped. Indians killed, 1.

October 13 .... Near Gageby Creek, Ind. Ter. Trs. H, K, and L, 8th U. S. Cav.; Indian Scouts. Maj. W. R. Price in command.

October 17 .... Near Washita River, Ind. Ter. Tr. I, 6th U. S. Cav. Capt. A. R. Chaffee in command. Surprised an Indian camp and destroyed their entire outfit.

October 21—November 8 .... Expedition from Ft. Sill, Ind. Ter. Tr. D, 6th U. S. Cav.; Trs. B, C, F, H, L, and M, 10th U. S. Cav.; Co. D, 5th U. S. Infty.; Cos. D, E, and I, 11th U. S. Infty.; Indian scouts. Lieut. Col. J. W. Davidson, 10th U. S. Cav., in command. Indians captured, 391. Indian ponies captured, 2000.

October 23 .... Old Pueblo Fork of Little Colorado, Ariz. Tr. A, 5th U. S. Cav.; and Detachment of Trs. I and A, 5th U. S. Cav.; and Indian Scouts. Lieut. Bernard Reilly, Jr., in command. Indians killed, 16. Indians captured, 1.

October 24 .... Elk Creek, Ind. Ter. Three Troops of 10th U. S. Cav. Maj. G. W. Schofield in command. Indians captured, 319. Horses captured, 1500 to 2000. Part of expedition from Ft. Sill.

October 29 .... Cave Creek, Ariz. Detachment of Tr. K, 5th U. S. Cav. Sergt. R. Stauffer in command. Indians killed, 8. Indians captured, 5.

November 1 .... Sunset Pass, Little Colorado River, Ariz. Detachments of Trs. A, and K, 5th U. S. Cav. Lieut. Chas. King in command. Lieut. King wounded. Indians killed, 1.

November 3 .... On Laguna Curato, Texas. Trs. A, D, E, F, H, I, K, and L, 4th U. S. Cav. Col. R. S. Mackenzie in command. Indians killed, 2. Indians captured, 19.

November 6 .... McClellan Creek, Texas. Tr. H, 8th U. S. Cav. Lieut. H. J. Farnsworth in command. Soldiers killed, 2. Soldiers wounded, 4. Indians killed, 4. Indians wounded, 10. 6 cavalry horses killed. Fight with 100 Southern Cheyennes.

November 6 .... Near Laguna Tahoka, Texas. Tr. A, 4th U. S. Cav. Lieut. W. A. Thompson in command. Indians killed, 2.

November 8 .... Near McClellan Creek, Texas. Detachment of Tr. D, 6th U. S. Cav.; Detachment of Co. D, 5th U. S. Infty. Lieut. F. D. Baldwin, 5th U. S. Infty., in command. Two children, Adelaide and Julia German, 5 and 7 years of age, rescued from the Indians.

November 8 .... Near McClellan, Texas. Trs. B, D, F, and H, 10th U. S. Cav.; Cos. E and I, 11th U. S. Infty. Capt. C. D. Viele, 10th U. S. Cav., in command. Sent after the Indians attacked by Lieut. Baldwin. Had several skirmishes and captured a number of ponies and mules.

November 10 .... Near Ft. Dodge, Kans. Detachment of Tr. B, 6th U. S. Cav.

November 25 .... Snow Lake, or Jarvis Pass, Ariz. Detachments of Trs. A and K, 5th U. S. Cav. Lieut. G. O. Eaton in command. Indians killed, 3. Indians captured, 9.

November 28 .... Near Muster Creek, Texas. Trs. C, H, K, and L, 8th U. S. Cav. Capt. C. A. Hartwell in command. Indians killed, 2. Indians wounded, 2.

December 1 .... Canon Creek, Tonto Basin, Ariz. Detachment of Tr. B, 5th U. S. Cav., and Indian Scouts. Capt. R. H. Montgomery in command. Indians killed, 8. Indians wounded, 2. Indians captured, 14.

December 2 .... Gageby Creek, Ind. Ter. Detachment of Tr. I, 6th U. S. Cav. Sergt. D. Ryan in command. Chased Indians for 10 miles, killing and capturing about 50 ponies.

December 7 .... Kingfisher Creek, Ind. Ter. Tr. D, 10th U. S. Cav., and Detachment of Tr. M, 10th U. S. Cav. Capt. A. S. B. Keyes in command. Attacked a band of Southern Cheyennes. Indians captured, 26.

December 8 .... Muchaquay Valley, Staked Plains, Texas. Tr. I, 4th U. S. Cav. Lieut. Mathew Leeper, jr., in command. Indians killed, 2. Indians captured, 1.

December 12 .... Standing Rock Agency, Dak. Trs. F, and L, 7th U. S. Cav. Capt. G. W. Yates in command.

December 20 .... Kingfisher Creek on North Fork of Canadian River, Ind. Ter. Tr. D and Detachment of Tr. M, 10th U. S. Cav., and Indian Scouts.

December 28 .... North Fork of Canadian River, Ind. Ter. Trs. I and M, 10th U. S. Cav. Capt. A. S. B. Keyes in command. Indians captured, 52.

1875

January 2 to February 23 .... Scout from Camp Apache, Ariz. Detachments of Trs. B and I and A, 5th U. S. Cav.; and Indian Scouts. Capt. F. D. Ogilby, 8th U. S. Cav., in command. Indians killed, 15. Indians captured, 122.

January 3—6 .... Hackberry Creek, Kans. Co. F, 5th U. S. Infty.; and Detachment of Co. K, 19th U. S. Infty. Lieut. F. S. Hinkle, 5th U. S. Infty., in command. Indians captured, 4.

January 9 .... Camp Apache, Ariz. Co. K, 8th U. S. Infty. Capt. W. S. Worth in command.

January 26 .... Solis Ranch, near Ringgold Barracks, Texas. Detachment of Tr. G, 9th U. S. Cav. Col. Edward Hatch in command. Soldiers killed, 2.

January 27 .... Near Ringgold Barracks, Texas. Trs. B, and G, 9th U. S. Cav. Col. Edward Hatch in command. Indians wounded, 2.

January 29 .... Sierra Ancho, Ariz. Detachment of Tr. K, 5th U. S. Cav.

February 23 .... On Salt Fork of Red River, Texas. Lieut. Col. J. W. Davidson, 10th U. S. Cav., in command. Captured band of Kiowas consisting of 65 men, and 175 women and children. 300 ponies and 70 mules also captured. Among the prisoners were Lone Wolf, Red Otter, and Lean Bull.

April 6 .... Near Cheyenne Agency, Ind. Ter. Tr. M, 6th U. S. Cav.; Trs. D and M, 10th U. S. Cav.; and Detachment of Co. H, 5th U. S. Infty. Lieut. Col. T. H. Neill, 6th U. S. Cav., in command. Soldiers wounded, 19. Indians killed, 11. Black Horse, Cheyenne Indian Chief, killed. A party of about 60 or 70 Cheyennes, consisting of the worse criminals of the tribe —those who had murdered the German family and others— being afraid on that account to surrender with the rest, crossed the Arkansas River west of Fort Dodge and attempted to make their way to the Sioux country, north of the Platte.

April 23 .... North fork of Sappa Creek, Kans. Detachments of Tr. H, 6th U. S. Cav.; and Detachments of Co. K, 19th U. S. Infty. Lieut. Austin Henely, 6th U. S. Cav., in command. Soldiers killed, 2. Indians killed, 27. 125 Indian ponies captured and the Indian camp burned.

April 25 .... Eagle Nest, crossing Pecos River, Texas. Seminole Negro Scouts from 24th U. S. Infty. Lieut. J. L. Bullis in command. Indians killed, 3. Indians wounded, 1. Troops attacked a band of 25 Comanches.

April 30 .... La Luz Canon, N. M. Tr. D, 8th U. S. Cav. Capt. J. F. Randlett in command. Indians captured, 9.

May 5 .... Battle Point, Texas. Detachments of Trs. A, F, G, I, and L, 10th U. S. Cav.; and Indian Scouts. Sergt. John Marshall in command. Indians wounded, 1.

June 1 .... Near Ft. Verde, Ariz. Indian Scouts.

June 3 .... Hackberry Creek, Ind. Ter. Detachment of Tr. A, 4th U. S. Cav. Lieut. J. A. McKinney in command. One Osage Indian killed. Indians caught robbing a cattle herd.

June 9—15 .... Tonto Basin, Ariz. Indian Scouts.

June 27 to July 8 .... Tonto Basin, Ariz. Cos. A and B, 8th U. S. Infty.; and Indian Scouts. Capt. G. M. Brayton, 8th U. S. Infty., in command. Soldiers wounded, 1. Indians killed, 30. Indians captured, 15.

June 29 .... Near Reynolds' Ranch, Texas. Tr. A, 4th U. S. Cav. Lieut. J. A. McKinney in command. Indians killed, 1.

July 1 .... Little Popo Agie River, Wyo. Detachment of Tr. D, 2nd U. S. Cav. Corp. R. W. Payne in command. Indians killed, 2.

July 6 .... Ponca Agency, Dakota. Detachment of Co. G, 1st U. S. Infty. Sergt. A. C. Danvers in command. Agency attacked by band of between 150 and 200 Sioux. Drove off Indians by loading an old cannon with pieces of iron in 3 assaults.

July 7 .... Near Camp Lewis, Mont. Detachments of Cos. G and K, 7th U. S. Infty. Lieut. G. H. Wright in command. Soldiers killed, 3. Band of 50 Indians ran off a quantity of horses. Troops recovered 7 head.

August 28 to September 2 .... North Platte River, north of Sidney, Nebr. Detachment of Tr. G, 3rd U. S. Cav. Lieut. Emmet Crawford in command.

October 27 .... Near Buffalo Station, or Smoky Hill Station, Kans. Detachment of Tr. H, 5th U. S. Cav. Capt. J. M. Hamilton in command. Soldiers wounded, 1. Indians killed, 2.

November 2 .... Near Pecos River, Texas. Trs. G and L, 10th U. S. Cav.; and Indian Scouts. Lieut. Andrew Geddes, 25th U. S. Infty., in command. Indians killed, 1. Indians captured, 5.

November 20 .... Near Antelope Station, Nebr. Detachment of Tr. G, 3rd U. S. Cav. Lieut. Emmet Crawford in command.

1876

January 9 .... Camp Apache, Ariz. Trs. A and D, 6th U. S. Cav.; Cos. E and K, 8th U. S. Infty.; and Co. A, Indian Scouts. Capt. F. D. Ogilby, 8th U. S. Infty., in command. Indians killed, 1. Indians captured, 5.

January 22 .... Cimarron River, 125 Miles east of Camp Supply, Ind. Ter. Detachment of Tr. G, 5th U. S. Cav. Lieut. H. S. Bishop in command. Indians killed, 3. Indians captured, 4. Captured 35 ponies and 2 mules.

February 1 .... Near Chevelons Fork, Ariz. Detachment of Co. A. Indian Scouts. Capt. F. D. Ogilby, 8th U. S. Infty., in command. Indians killed, 4. Indians captured, 6.

February 18 .... Carrizo Mountains, Texas. Detachment of Co. B, 25th U. S. Infty. Capt. Chas. Bentzoni in command.

February 22 to March 17 .... Fort Pease, trading post, Mont. Trs. F, G, H, and L, 2nd U. S. Cav.; Detachment of Co. C, 7th U. S. Infty. Maj. J. S. Brisbin, 2nd U. S. Cav., in command. Citizens killed, 6. Citizens wounded, 8. Troops went from Ft. Ellis to the relief of the men at the trading post. 19 of the men rescued.

March 5 .... Dry forks of Powder River, Wyo. Cos. C and I, 4th U. S. Infty., (Crook's Big Horn Expedition.) Capt. E. M. Coates in command. Soldiers wounded, 1.

March 17 .... Crazy Horse's Camp on Little Powder River, Mont. Trs. A, B, E, I, and K, 2nd U. S. Cav.; Trs. A, D, E, F, and M, 3rd U. S. Cav., (Crook's Big Horn Expedition) Col. J. J. Reynolds, 3rd U. S. Cav., in command. Soldiers killed, 4. Lieut. W. C. Rawolle, 2nd U. S. Cav., wounded. Soldiers wounded, 5. 105 Indian Lodges destroyed. The village was a perfect magazine of ammunition, war material, and general supplies, and every evidence was found to prove these Indians in copartnership with those at the Red Cloud and Spotted Tail Agencies, that the proceeds of raids upon settlements had been taken into those agencies and supplies brought out in return.

March 27—28 .... Tonto Basin, Ariz. Detachment of Co. A, Indian Scouts. Guide E. Stanley in command. Indians killed, 16.

April .... Central Station, Texas. Detachment of Co. D, 25th U. S. Infty. Sergt. W. Smith in command. Citizens killed, 1.

April 10 .... San Jose Mountains, Ariz., near Sonora line. Detachment of Tr. H, 6th U. S. Cav. Lieut. Austin Henely in command.

April 13 .... Near Ft. Sill, Ind. Ter. Detachment of Tr. I, 4th U. S. Cav. Lieut. O. W. Budd in command. Indians captured, 6.

April 28 .... Grace Creek, Nebr. Detachment of Co. A, 23rd U. S. Infty. Lieut. C. H. Heyl in command. Soldiers killed, 1. Indians killed, 1. Indians wounded, 1.

June 9 .... Tongue River, Wyo. Trs. A, B, C, D, E, F, G, I, L, and M, 3rd U. S. Cav.; Trs. A, B, D, E, and I, 2nd U. S. Cav.; Cos. D and F, 4th U. S. Infty.; Cos. C, G, and H, 9th U. S. Infty. Lieut. Col. W. B. Royall, 3rd U. S. Cav., in command. (Crook's Expedition.) Soldiers wounded, 1.

June 17 .... Rosebud River, Mont. Trs. A, B, D, E, and I, 2nd U. S. Cav.; Trs. A, B, C, D, E, F, H, I, L, and M, 3rd U. S. Cav.; Cos. D and F, 4th U. S. Infty.; Cos. C, G, and H, 9th U. S. Infty. Brig. Gen. Geo. Crook in command. Soldiers killed, 9. Capt. G. V. Henry, 3rd U. S. Cav., wounded. Soldiers wounded, 20. Indians killed, 11.

June 22 .... Elkhorn River, Nebr. Tr. K, 2nd U. S. Cav. Capt. James Egan in command. Indians killed, 1.

June 25 .... Little Big Horn River, Mont. Attack on Crazy Horse's and Sitting Bull's bands of Sioux Indians. Trs. C, E, F, I, and L, 7th U. S. Cav. Lieut. Col. G. A. Custer in command. Officers killed, Lieut. Col. G. A. Custer; Capts. T. W. Custer, G. W. Yates, and M. W. Keogh; Lieuts. W. W. Cooke, A. E. Smith, James Calhoun, J. E. Potter, H. M. Harrington, J. G. Sturgis, and W. V. W. Reily, 7th U. S. Cav.; and Lieut. J. J. Crittenden, 20th U. S. Infty., and Asst. Surg. G. E. Lord. Citizens killed, 4. Soldiers killed, 189.

June 25—26 .... Little Big Horn River, Mont. Trs. A, B, D, G, H, K, and M, 7th U. S. Cav. Maj. M. A. Reno in command. Officers killed: Lieuts. Donald McIntosh, and B. H. Hodgson, and Actg. Asst. Surg. J. M. DeWolf. Soldiers killed, 46. Citizens killed, 1. Officers wounded; Capt. F. W. Benteen and Lieut. C. A. Varnum. Soldiers wounded, 44.

July 7 .... Head of Tongue River, Mont. Detachments of Trs. A, B, D, and I, 2nd U. S. Cav. Lieut. F. W. Sibley in command. Indians wounded, 5.

July 17 .... Near War Bonnet or Hat Creek or Indian Creek, Wyo. Trs. A, B, D, G, I, K, and M, 5th U. S. Cav. Col. Wesley Merritt in command. Intercepted a band of about 800 Indians and chased the entire band back to the Red Cloud Agency. Indians killed, 1. Indians wounded, 1.

July 17—18 .... Near Hat Creek, Wyo. Detachment of Tr. K, 3rd U. S. Cav.

July 29 .... Mouth of Powder River, Mont. Cos. E, F, G, H, I, and K, 22nd U. S. Infty. Lieut. Col. E. S. Otis in command. Soldiers wounded, 1.

July 30 .... Near Saragossa, Mexico. Detachment of Co. B, 10th U. S. Cav.; and Indian Scouts. Lieut. J. L. Bullis, 24th U. S. Infty., in command. Struck a band of hostile Lipans and Kickapoos. Indians killed, 12. Indians captured, 4.

August 1 .... Red Canon, Mont. Co. K, 4th U. S. Infty. Capt. W. S. Collier in command.

August 2 .... Near Mouth of Rosebud River, Mont. Two companies of 6th U. S. Infty.; and one company of 17th U. S. Infty. Maj. O. H. Moore, 6th U. S. Infty., in command. Soldiers killed, 1. Indians killed, 1.

August 14 .... Near Ft. Buford, Dak. Steamer loaded with troops fired on by Indians. Troops returned the fire and the Indians fled. No casualties.

August 15 .... Red Rock Country, Ariz. Detachment of Tr. E, 6th U. S. Cav., and Indian Scouts. Capt. Chas. Porter, 8th U. S. Infty., in command. Soldiers wounded, 1. Indians killed, 7. Indians captured, 7.

August 23 .... Near mouth of Yellowstone River, Mont. Co. G, 6th U. S. Infty. Guard on steamers "Josephine" and "Benton." Lieut. Nelson Bronson in command. Soldiers killed, 1.

September 9 .... Slim Buttes, Dak. Surprise of "American Horse." Trs. A, B, D, E, and I, 2nd U. S. Cav.; Trs. A, B, C, D, E, F, G, I, L, and M, 3rd U. S. Cav.; Trs. A, B, C, D, E, F, G, I, K, and M, 5th U. S. Cav.; Cos. D, F, and G, 4th U. S. Infty.; Cos. C, G, and H, 9th U. S. Infty.; Cos. B, C, F, and I, 14th U. S. Infty. Lieut. Col. E. A. Carr, 5th U. S. Cav., in command of the troops. Gen. George Crook in charge of the expedition. Soldiers killed, 2. Citizens killed, 1. Lieut. A. H. Van Luettwitz, 3rd U. S. Cav., wounded. Soldiers wounded, 13. Captured village of 37 lodges, quantities of supplies, arms and ammunition, and about 175 ponies. Among the articles taken from the village were a guidon of the 7th Cavalry, a pair of gloves marked with the name of Col. Keogh and other things which belonged to Custer's command. Indians killed, 4. "American Horse" was mortally wounded. Indians captured, 12.

September 14 .... Owl Creek, Belle Fourche River, Dak. Two men, Privates Mose Milner and C. Madsen, of 5th U. S. Cav., were out hunting game for the troops. Milner met a party of Indians who immediately murdered him. Detachments of Trs. A, B, C, D, E, F, G, I, and K, 5th U. S. Cav., under Major J. J. Upham, arrived shortly after.

September 15 .... Florida Mountains, N. M. Tr. F, 9th U. S. Cav. Capt. Henry Carroll in command. Soldiers wounded, 1. Indians killed, 1. Captured 11 head of stock.

September 18 .... Caves east of Verde, Ariz. Detachment of Co. B, Indian Scouts. Guide Al Seiber in command. Indians killed, 5. Indians captured, 13.

October 4 .... Tonto Basin, Ariz. Detachments of Co. E, 6th U. S. Cav.; Indian Scouts. Capt. Chas. Porter, 8th U. S. Infty., in command. Indians killed, 8. Indians captured, 2.

October 9 .... Eagle Springs, Texas. Citizens killed, 1.

October 10 .... Near mouth of Glendive Creek, Mont. Cos. H, G, and K, 22nd U. S. Infty., Co. C, 15th U. S. Infty. Capt. C. W. Miner, 22nd U. S. Infty., in command. Escort for 49 wagons. From 400 to 600 Indians attacked the night camp.

October 14 .... Chugwater, or Richard Creek, Wyo. Detachment of Tr. K, 2nd U. S. Cav. Capt. James Egan in command. Soldiers killed, 1.

October 15 .... Clear Creek, Mont. Cos. G, H, and Detachments of Cos. I and K, 22nd U. S. Infty.; Cos. C and G, 17th U. S. Infty. Lieut. Col. E. S. Otis, 22nd U. S. Infty., in command. Soldiers wounded, 3.

October 21 .... Big Dry River, or Cedar Creek, Mont. 5th U. S. Infty. Col. N. A. Miles in command. Soldiers wounded, 2. Indians killed, 5.

October 23 .... Chadron Creek, near Camp Robinson, Nebr. Trs. B, D, E, F, I, and M, 4th U. S. Cav.; Trs. H and L, 5th U. S. Cav.; and Indian Scouts. Col. R. S. Mackenzie in command. Indians captured, 400. Captured Red Cloud and Red Leaf's bands.

October 27 .... Big Dry River, Mont. Surrender of Sioux Indians. Col. N. A. Miles, 5th U. S. Infty., in command. Indians captured, 2000.

November 25—26 .... Bates Creek, near North Fork of Powder River, Wyo. Tr. K, 2nd U. S. Cav.; Trs. H and K, 3rd U. S. Cav.; Trs. B, D, E, F, I, and M, 4th U. S. Cav.; Trs. H and L, 5th U. S. Cav. Col. R. S. Mackenzie, 4th U. S. Cav., in command. Lieut. J. A. McKinney, 4th U. S. Cav., killed. Soldiers killed, 5. Soldiers wounded, 25. Indians killed, 25. "Dull Knife's" village of 173 lodges and all its contents was entirely destroyed. About 500 ponies were captured.

December 7 .... Bark Creek, Mont. Cos. G, H, and I, 5th U. S. Infty. Lieut. F. D. Baldwin in command.

December 18 .... Near head of Red Water Creek, Dak. Cos. G, H, and I, 5th U. S. Infty. Lieut. F. D. Baldwin in command.

1877

January 1—3 .... Valley of the Tongue River, Wyo. Cos. A, C, D, E, K, 5th U. S. Infty.; Cos. E and F, 22nd U. S. Infty. Col. N. A. Miles in command. Drove the Indians up the valley.

January 7 .... Valley of the Tongue River, Wyo. Cos. A, C, D, E, K, 5th U. S. Infty.; Cos. E and F, 22nd U. S. Infty. Col. N. A. Miles in command. Troops captured a young warrior and 7 Cheyenne women and children.

January 8 .... Wolf Mountains, Mont. Cos. A, C, D, E, K, and Detachments of Cos. B and H, 5th U. S. Infty.; Cos. E and F, 22nd U. S. Infty. Col. N. A. Miles, 5th U. S. Infty., in command. Soldiers killed, 3. Soldiers wounded, 8.

January 9 .... Leitendorf range of mountains, N. M. Detachments of Cos. H and L, 6th U. S. Cav.; and Co. C, Indian Scouts. Lieut. J. A. Rucker, 6th U. S. Cav., in command. Soldiers wounded, 1. Indians killed, 10. Indians captured, 1.

January 9—February 5 .... Scout in Tonto Basin, Ariz. Detachment of Cos. E and B, 6th U. S. Cav.; Indian Scouts. Capt. G. M. Brayton, 8th U. S. Infty., in command. Indians killed, 18. Indians captured, 20.

January 12 .... Near Elkhorn Creek, Wyo. Detachment of Tr. A, 3rd U. S. Cav. Lieut. H. H. Wright in command. Soldiers wounded, 3.

January 23 .... Florida Mountains, N. M. Detachment of Tr. C, 9th U. S. Cav. Lieut. H. H. Wright in command.

January 28 .... Siena Boca Grande, Mexico. Detachment of Tr. C, 9th U. S. Cav. Capt. C. D. Beyer in command.

February 22 .... Staked Plains, Texas. Citizens killed, 1.

February 23 .... Hay Creek, near Deadwood, Dak. Tr. C, 3rd U. S. Cav. Lieut. J. F. Cummings in command. Indians killed, 1. Recaptured 600 sheep, 17 horses, and 7 head of cattle.

March 7 .... Near Ft. Davis, Texas. Citizens killed, 2.

April 1 .... Rio Grande, near Devil's River, Texas. Seminole Negro Scouts. Lieut. J. L. Bullis, 24th U. S. Infty., in command.

April and May .... Red Cloud and Spotted Tail Agencies. Indian surrender. Gen. Geo. Crook in command. Indians captured, 2300. Col. R. S. Mackenzie, 4th U. S. Cav., and Pawnee Scouts were present.

April 20—22 .... Ft. Clark, Texas. Citizens killed, 3.

May 4 .... Lake Quemado, Texas. Tr. G, 10th U. S. Cav.; Indian Scouts. Capt. P. L. Lee, 10th U. S. Cav., in command. Soldiers killed, 1. Indians killed, 4. Indians captured, 6. 69 head of stock recaptured, 12 lodges with their contents destroyed.

May 6 .... Canon Resecata. Tr. G, 10th U. S. Cav.; Indian Scouts. Capt. P. L. Lee, 10th U. S. Cav., in command. 3 lodges and their supplies burned.

May 7 .... Little Muddy Creek, Mont. Trs. F, G, H, and K, 2nd U. S. Cav.; Cos. B and H, 5th U. S. Infty.; Cos. E, F, G, and H, 22nd U. S. Infty. Col. N. A. Miles, 5th U. S. Infty., in command. Soldiers killed, 4. Lieut. Alfred M. Fuller, 2nd U. S. Cav., wounded. Soldiers wounded, 7. Indians killed, 30. Indians wounded, 20. Indians captured, 40. Chief Lame Deer and his head warrior, Iron Star, were killed. 450 horses, mules, and ponies, captured. 51 lodges well stocked with supplies were captured.

May 29 .... Near Camp Bowie, Ariz. Tr. H and L, 6th U. S. Cav. Lieut. Frank West in command.

May 30 .... Near Ft. Davis, Texas. Citizens killed, 1.

June 15 to October 5 .... Nez Perces Campaign. Gen. O. O. Howard in command.

June 15 .... John Day's Creek, Idaho. Citizens killed, 4.

June 17 .... White Bird Canon, Idaho. Trs. F and H, 1st U. S. Cav. Capt. David Perry in command. Lieut. E. R. Theller, 21st U. S. Infty., killed. Soldiers killed, 33. Soldiers wounded, 1.

June 28 .... White Bird River, Idaho. Trs. F and H, 1st U. S. Cav.; Bat. A, D, G, and M, 4th U. S. Artillery; Co. C, 21st U. S. Infty. Gen. O. O. Howard in command.

July 1—3 .... Cottonwood Ranch on Clearwater River, Idaho. Tr. E and L, 1st U. S. Cav. Nez Perces Expedition. Capt. S. G. Whipple in command. Lieut. S. M. Rains, 1st U. S. Cav., killed July 3. Soldiers killed, 10. Citizens killed, 2. This is as the Adjutant General's Report gives it. Heitman gives it: July 1 .... Clearwater River, Idaho. Trs. E, L, 1st U. S. Cav. Capt. S. G. Whipple in command. July 3 .... Near Craig's Mts., Idaho. Detachment of Tr. L, 1st U. S. Cav. Lieut. S. M. Rains in command. Lieut. Rains, killed.

July 4—5 .... Cottonwood Ranch on Clearwater, Idaho. Trs. E, F, and L, 1st U. S. Cav.; and citizens. Nez Perces Expedition. Capt. David Perry in command. Soldiers wounded, 2.

July 4 .... Norton's Ranch, Idaho. Nez Perces Expedition. Skirmish. Gen. Howard's report.

July 11—12 .... South Fork of Clearwater, Idaho. Trs. B, D, F, H, and L, 1st U. S. Cav,; Cos. A, B, C, D, E, H, and I, 21st U. S. Infty.; Bat. A, D, E, and G, 4th U. S. Artillery. Nez Perces Expedition. Gen. O. O. Howard in command. Soldiers killed, 13. Capt. E. A. Bancroft, 4th Art., and Lieut. C. A. Williams, 21st U. S. Infty., wounded. Soldiers wounded, 25. Indians killed, 23. Indians wounded, 46. Indians captured, 40.

July 13 .... Kamiah, Idaho. Trs. B, F, H, and L, 1st U. S. Cav.; Cos. A, B, C, D, E, H, and I, 21st U. S. Infty.; Bats. A, D, E, and G, 4th U. S. Artillery. Nez Perces Expedition. Gen. O. O. Howard in command.

July 17 .... Weippe, Oro Fino Creek, Idaho. Detachments of Trs. B, E, H, and L, 1st U. S. Cav.; Indian Scouts; and McConville Vols. Nez Perces Expedition. Maj. E. C. Mason, 21st U. S. Infty., in command. Soldiers killed, 1. Soldiers wounded, 1. Indians killed, 1.

July 21 .... Belle Fourche, Dak. Detachments of Trs. A, D, E, F, and G, 3rd U. S. Cav. Lieut. H. R. Lemly in command.

August 1 .... Near El Muerto, Texas. Citizens killed, 2.

August 9—10 .... Big Hole Basin, Mont. Detachments of Trs. B and E, 2nd U. S. Cav.; Cos. A, D, F, G, I, and K, 7th U. S. Infty.; Citizen volunteers. Nez Perces Expedition. Col. John Gibbon, 7th U. S. Infty., in command. Capt. Wm. Logan and 1st Lieut. J. H. Bradley killed. Col. John Gibbon, Capt. Constant Williams, and Lieuts. C. A. Coolidge, W. S. English and C. A. Woodruff, wounded. All of 7th U. S. Infty. Soldiers killed, 21. Citizens killed, 6. Soldiers wounded, 31. Citizens wounded, 4. Indians killed, 89.

August 20 .... Camas Meadows, Idaho. Trs. B, C, I, and K, 1st U. S. Cav.; Tr. L, 2nd U. S. Cav.; Detachment of Bat. E, 4th U. S. Artillery; Co. H, 8th U. S. Infty. Maj. G. B. Sanford, 1st U. S. Cav., in command. Soldiers killed, 1. Lieut. H. M. Benson, 7th U. S. Infty., wounded. Soldiers wounded, 6.

August 29 .... Near Black Rock Ariz. Detachment of Tr. F, 6th U. S. Cav. Lieut. G. E. Overton in command. Indians captured, 13.

September 8—10 .... Near San Francisco River and Mogollon

Mountains, N. M. Detachment of Trs. B and M, 6th U. S Cav.; Indian Scouts. Capt. T. C. Tupper, 6th U. S. Cav., in command. Indians killed, 12. Indians captured, 13.

September 13 .... Canon Creek, Mont. Nez Perces Expedition. Tr. K, 1st U. S. Cav.; Detachments of Trs. C and I, 1st U. S. Cav.; Trs. F, G, H, I, L, and M, 7th U. S. Cav. Col. S. D. Sturgis, 7th U. S. Cav., in command. Soldiers killed, 3. Capt. T. H. French, 7th U. S. Cav., wounded. Soldiers wounded, 10. Indians killed, 21. Indians lost about 900 ponies.

September 23 .... Cow Island, Mont. Detachment of Co. B, 7th U. S. Infty. and citizen volunteers. Sergt. Wm. Molchart in command. Soldiers killed, 1. Citizens killed, 2. Nez Perces Campaign.

September 25 .... Near Cow Creek Canon, Mont. Citizens volunteers. Major Guido Ilges, 7th U. S. Infty., in command. Citizens killed, 1. Indians wounded, 2. Nez Perce Campaign.

September 26 .... Saragossa, Mexico. Detachments of Tr. A and F, 8th U. S. Cav.; Detachment of Tr. C, 10th U. S. Cav. Lieut. J. L. Bullis, 24th U. S. Infty., in command. Indians captured, 5.

September 30 .... Snake or Eagle Creek, near Bear Paw Mountains, Mont. Tr. F, G, and H, 2nd U. S. Cav.; Trs. A, D, and K, 7th U. S. Cav.; Cos. B, F, G, I, and K, Detachment of Co. D, 5th U. S. Infty. (mounted) ; Indian Scouts. Col. N. A. Miles, 5th U. S. Infty., in command. Capt. Owen Hale and Lieut. J. W. Biddle, 7th U. S. Cav., killed. Capt. Myles Moylan and E. S. Godfrey, 7th U. S. Cav., and Lieuts. G. W. Baird and Henry Romeyn, 5th U. S. Infty., wounded. Soldiers killed, 22. Soldiers wounded, 38. Citizens wounded, 8. Indians killed, 17. Indians wounded, 40.

October 4—5 .... Bear Paw Mountains, near Snake Creek, Mont. Surrender of the Nez Perces Indians. Indians captured, 418.

October 22 .... Flat Rocks, Texas. Citizens killed, 1.

November 1 .... Big Bend of Rio Grande, Texas. Seminole Negro Scouts. Lieut. J. L. Bullis, 24th U. S. Infty., in command. Fight was with the Apaches.

November 16 .... Near Indian Creek, Texas. Citizens killed, 1.

November 18 .... Near Sauz Ranch, Texas. Citizens killed, 2.

November 29—30 .... Sierra Carmel Ranch, Mexico. Trs. A and K, 8th U. S. Cav.; Tr. C, 10th U. S. Cav.; and Indian Scouts. Capt. S. B. M. Young, 8th U. S. Cav., in command. Soldiers wounded, 1. Indians killed, 2. Indians wounded, 3.

December 13 .... Ralston Flat, N. M. Detachments of Trs. C, G, H, and L, 6th U. S. Cav.; and Indian Scouts. Lieut. J. A. Rucker, 6th U. S. Cav., in command. Indians killed, 1.

December 18 .... Las Animas Mountains, Mexico. Detachments of Trs. C, G, H, and L, 6th U. S. Cav.; and Indian Scouts. Lieut. J. A. Rucker, 6th U. S. Cav., in command. Indians killed, 15. Indians captured, 1.

December 23 .... Bass Canon, near Van Horn's Wells, Texas. Citizens killed, 2.

January 5 .... Presidio del Norte, Texas. (63 miles northwest.) 6
citizens killed by Mescalero Apaches from the Ft. Stanton,
Reservation, N. M.

January 7 .... Near Tonto Creek, Ariz. Tr. A, 6th U. S. Cav.; Co.
B, 8th U. S. Infty.; Co. B, Indian Scouts. Capt. Chas. Porter,
8th U. S. Infty., in command. Indians killed, 3.

January 16 .... Mason County, Texas. Citizens killed, 2.

January 16 .... Brady City, Texas. Citizens killed, 1.

January 16 .... Ross Fork Agency, Idaho. Trs. B, F, and I, 5th U. S.
Cav.; Cos. C, D, E, and G, 14th U. S. Infty. Col. J. E. Smith,
14th U. S. Infty., in command. Indians captured, 10. 250
horses captured. Troops surprised a party of Bannocks.

January 16 .... Russell's Ranch, on the Rio Grande, Texas. Tr. H,
10th U. S. Cav.; Cos. A, and H, 25th U. S. Infty. Capt. M.
L. Courtney, 25th U. S. Infty., in command. Citizens killed,
4. Citizens wounded, 3.

February 5 .... Headwaters of Sunday Creek, Montana. Indian
Scouts from Fort Keogh. Indians killed, 1.

February 13 .... Near Fort Keogh, Montana. Indian Scouts from
Fort Peck. Soldiers killed, 1. Indians wounded, 1.

February 16 .... Point of Rocks, Limpia Canon, Texas. Citizens
killed, 2.

February 23 .... Laredo Road, below Ft. Duncan, Texas. Citizens
killed, 2.

February 23 .... Near Ft. Keogh, Mont. Indian Scouts.

April 5 .... Mogollon Mountains, Ariz. Detachment of Tr. A, 6th
U. S. Cav.; Detachment of Co. B, 8th U. S. Infty.; Indian
Scouts. Capt. Chas. Porter, 8th U. S. Infty., in command.
Indians killed, 7. Indians captured, 7.

April 15 .... Carrizo Mountains, Texas. Detachment of Tr. K, 10th
U. S. Cav. Lieut. A. Geddes, 25th U. S. Infty., in command.
Pursued a band of Mescalero Apache Indians.

April 15 .... Near Escondido Station, Texas. Detachment of Tr. B,
10th U. S. Cav. Lieut. John Bigelow in command. Citizens
killed, 1.

April 17 .... Steele's Ranch, Nueces River, Texas. Citizens killed, 2.
Killed by Lipan and Kickapoo Indians.

April 17 .... Near Ft. Quitman, Texas. Citizens killed, 1.

April 17 .... San Ygnacio, Texas. Citizens killed, 1.

April 17 .... Near Brown's Ranch, Texas. Citizens killed, 1.

April 18 .... Rancho Soledad, Texas. Citizens killed, 3.

April 18 .... Charco Escondido, Texas. Citizens killed, 1.

April 19 .... Quijotes Gordes, Texas. Citizens killed, 1.

April 19 .... Charco Escondido, Texas. Citizens killed, 1.

April 20 .... Point of Rocks, near Ft. Davis, Texas. One mail rider
and 2 citizens killed by Mescalero Apaches from Ft. Stanton
Reservation, N. M.

May 20 .... Smith's Mills, near Wickenburg, Ariz. Detachment of
Tr. I, 6th U. S. Cav. Lieut. E. E. Dravo in command. Indians
captured, 17.

May 20 .... Head of White's Gulch, Mont. Detachments of Cos. D,
and E, 7th U. S. Infty. Capt. Walter Clifford in command.

Indians killed, 1. Indians wounded, 2.

May 30 to Sept. .... Bannock Campaign. Gen. O. O. Howard in command.

June 1 .... Camp Wood, 12 miles west of, Texas. Two herders killed.

June 23 .... Silver River, Ore. Trs. A, F, G, and L, 1st U. S. Cav. Capt. R. F. Bernard in command. Soldiers killed, 3. Soldiers wounded, 2. Indians killed, 5. Indians wounded, 2.

June 28 .... Ft. Sill, Ind. Ter. A United States marshal, with a guard of soldiers. Lieut. S. R. Whitall, 16th U. S. Infty., in command. Soldiers attempted to execute a writ for the arrest of some Indians. Indians resisted. Indians killed, 2. Indians wounded, 1.

June 30 .... On the South Concho River, Texas. Detachment of Tr. D, 10th U. S. Cav. Lieut. C. R. Ward in command.

July 8 .... Birch Creek, Ore. (Bannock Campaign) Trs. A, E, F, G, H, K, and L, 1st U. S. Cav. Gen. O. O. Howard in command. Soldiers killed, 1. Soldiers wounded, 4.

July 8 .... Upper Columbia River. 10 men of Ordnance Department; 10 men of 21st U. S. Infty.

July 12 .... Ladd's Canon, Ore. (Bannock Campaign) Co. C, 12th U. S. Infty. Capt. J. L. Viven in command. Indians captured, 21.

July 13 .... Umatilla Agency, Ore. (Bannock Campaign) Tr. K, 1st U. S. Cav.; Bat. G and D, 4th U. S. Artillery; Cos. B, D, E, G, H, I, and K, 21st U. S. Infty. Capt. Evan Miles, 21st U. S. Infty., in command. Soldiers wounded, 2. Fight with Piute and Bannock Indians.

July 15 .... Near Meachan's Ranch Ore., Trs. D. and L, 1st U. S. Cav. Fight with Bannock Indians.

July 20 .... North Fork of John Day's River, Ore. Trs. A, E, F, G, H, and L, 1st U. S. Cav. Lieut. Col. J. W. Forsyth in command. Citizens killed, 1. Soldiers wounded, 1. Citizens wounded, 1. Engagement with Bannock Indians.

July 21 .... Middle Fork of Clearwater River, Mont. Detachments of Cos. B, H, and I, 3rd U. S. Infty. Lieut. T. S. Wallace in command. Indians killed, 6. Indians wounded, 3. Indians captured, 31. Horses captured, 31.

July 26 .... Baker City, Idaho. Co. C and Detachment of Co. K, 2nd U. S. Infty. Capt. W. F. Drum in command.

July 29 .... Sacramento Mountains, Ariz. Navajo Indian Scouts. Lieut. H. H. Wright, 9th U. S. Cav., in command. Indians killed, 3. Indians wounded, 3. Indians captured, 1.

August 2 .... Guadaloupe Mountains, Texas. Detachment of Tr. H, 10th U. S. Cav. Serg. Claggett in command. Citizens killed, 1.

August 5 .... Dog Canon, N. M. Trs. F and H, 9th U. S. Cav.; Indian Scouts. Capt. Henry Carroll, 9th U. S. Cav., in command. Indians killed, 3. Indians wounded, 2. Indians captured, 1.

August 9 .... Bennett Creek, Idaho. (Bannock Campaign) Detachment of Co. K, 12th U. S. Infty. Capt. W. E. Dove in command. Soldiers wounded, 1.

August 27 .... Henry's Lake, Idaho. Tr. K, 2nd U. S. Cav. Capt. James Egan in command. Captured 56 head of stock.

August 29—30 .... Index Peak, Wyo. (Bannock Campaign.) Detachment of 5th U. S. Infty., and Indian Scouts. Lieut. W. P. Clark, 2nd U. S. Cav., in command.

September 4 .... Clark's Fork, Mont. Cos. A, C, F, G, I, and K, 5th U. S. Infty.; Indian Scouts. Col. N. A. Miles in command. Capt. A. S. Bennett killed. Citizens killed, 1. Soldiers wounded, 2. Indians killed, 11. Indians captured, 31. Captured 200 horses and mules.

September 12 .... Near Big Wind or Snake River, Wyo. Detachment of Tr. G, 5th U. S. Cav.; and Indian Scouts. Lieut. H. S. Bishop, 5th U. S. Cav., in command. Indians killed, 1.

September 13 .... Near Turkey Springs, Ind. Ter. Trs. G and H, 4th U. S. Cav. Capt. Joseph Rendlebrock in command. Soldiers killed, 2. Soldiers wounded, 1.

September 14 .... Red Hill, Ind. Ter. Trs. G and H, 4th U. S. Cav. Capt. Joseph Rendlebrock in command. Soldiers killed, 1.

September 17 .... Bear Creek, N. M. Co. D, Indian Scouts. Lieut. H. P. Perrine, 6th U. S. Cav., in command. Soldiers killed, 1. Indians killed, 2.

September 18 .... Near Bear or Bluff Creek, Kans. Tr. I, 4th U. S. Cav. Capt. W. C. Hemphill in command. Soldiers wounded, 1.

September 21—22 .... Sand Creek, Kans. Trs. F, G, H, and I, 4th U. S. Cav.; Co. A, 16th U. S. Infty.; Detachment of Co. F, 19th U. S. Infty.; and citizens. Capt. Joseph Rendlebrock, 4th U. S. Cav., in command.

September 27 .... Punished Woman's Fork, Kans. Detachments of Trs. B, F, G, H, and I, 4th U. S. Cav.; Cos. D, F, and G, 19th U. S. Infty. Lieut. Col. W. H. Lewis, 19th U. S. Infty., in command. Lieut. Col. W. H. Lewis wounded, September 27, died on September 28, 1878. Soldiers killed, 1. Soldiers wounded, 5.

October 5 .... Johnson's Fork of the Guadalupe, Texas. Citizens killed, 4.

October 22 .... Near Ft. Benton, Mont. Detachment of troops from Ft. Benton. Major G. Ilges, 7th U. S. Infty., in command. Captured a camp of 35 Indians, 80 horses and 14 guns.

October 22 .... Near Flat Rocks, Texas. Citizens killed, 1.

October 23 .... Sand Hills, Mont. Trs. B and D, 3rd U. S. Cav. Capt. J. B. Johnson in command. Indians captured, 149. 140 head of stock captured. Chiefs "Dull Knife," "Old Crow," and "Wild Hog" were among the prisoners.

November 27 .... Ft. Ellis, Mont. "Ten Doy," a friendly Indian, arrested 7 hostile Bannocks.

1879

January 9—22 .... Ft. Robinson, Nebr. (Revolt of Cheyenne Indians) Trs. A, C, E, F, H, and L, 3rd U. S. Cav. Capt. H. W. Wessells, Jr., commanding post. Soldiers killed, 7. Capt. H. W. Wessels, Jr., wounded, Jan. 22, 1879. Soldiers wounded, 13. Indians killed, 32. Indians captured, 71. "Dull Knife" killed,

January 15 .... Cormedos Mountains, N. M. Tr. A, 9th U. S. Cav.
Lieut. M. W. Day in command.

January 20 .... Near Bluff Station, Wyo. Trs. B and D, 3rd U. S.
Cav. Major A. W. Evans in command.

March 8 .... Ojo Caliente, N. M. Tr. I, 9th U. S. Cav. Lieut. C. W.
Merritt in command. "Victoria," with 22 Warm Spring
Apache Indians, surrendered to Lieut. Merritt.

March 15 .... Ft. Ewell, Texas. (50 miles from) Citizens killed, 1.

March 25 .... Box Elder Creek, Mont. Trs. E. and I, 2nd U. S. Cav.;
and Indian Scouts. Lieut. W. P. Clark, 2nd U. S. Cav., in
command. Indians captured, 114. "Little Wolf" and his
band of Northern Cheyennes surrendered. Surrendered 35
lodges and 150 ponies.

April 5 .... Mizpah Creek, Mont. Detachment of Tr. E, 2nd U. S.
Cav.; and Signal Corps. Sergeant of Signal Corps and one
man. Soldiers killed, 1. Soldiers wounded, 1.

April 6 .... Near Powder River, Mont. Soldiers killed, 1. Soldiers
wounded, 1. Indians were Gros Ventres.

April 10 .... Near Ft. Keogh, Mont. Detachment of Tr. B, 2nd U. S.
Cav.; and Indian Scouts. Sergt. T. B. Glover in command.
Indians captured, 8.

April 10 .... Young's Point, Mont. Indians attempted to steal stock
but were driven off.

April 14 .... Pryor's Fork, Mont. 7 horses stolen by Indians.

April 17 .... Near Careless Creek, Musselshell River, Mont. Detachment of Co. K, 3rd U. S. Infty.; Detachments of Cos. E and D,
7th U. S. Infty.; and Indian Scouts. Lieut. S. H. Loder, 7th
U. S. Infty., in command. Soldiers killed, 2. Soldiers wounded, 1. Indians killed, 8.

April 22 .... Countryman's Ranch, Mont. Indian Scouts. Indians
killed, 1. Scouts overtook a party of Sioux.

April 30 .... Ojo Caliente, N. M. Indian Scout couriers. Indians
killed, 1.

May 1 .... Between Ft. Ewell and Corpus Christi, Texas. Teamster
killed.

May 18 .... Near Van Horn's Wells, Texas. John Clarkson was
murdered.

May 29 .... Black Range of Mimbres Mountains, N. M. Detachments
of Trs. C and I, 9th U. S. Cav. Capt. C. D. Beyer in command.
Soldiers killed, 1. Soldiers wounded, 2. Troops attacked
Victoria's Apaches, captured the camp with all the animals.
Indians wounded, 4. Band escaped into Old Mexico.

June 1 .... Near Camp Wood, Texas. Citizens killed, 3.

June 19 .... Near Ft. Benton, Mont. Detachment of 8 men. Lieut. J.
T. Van Orsdale, 7th U. S. Infty., in command. Indians killed, 1.

June 25 .... Tonto Basin, Ariz. Co. B, Indian Scouts. Lieut. Fred
Von Schrader, 12th U. S. Infty., in command. Indians killed,
6. Indians captured, 1.

June 29 .... Alkali Creek, Mont. Crow Indian Scouts. Soldiers
killed, 1. Soldiers wounded, 4. Indians killed, 4. Captured 33 ponies.

June 30 .... Headwaters of North Concho River, Texas. Citizens killed, 1.

July 14 .... Near Ft. Clark, Texas. Citizens killed, 1.

July 17 .... Milk River, Mont. (Miles' Sioux Expedition) Trs. A, B, C, E, G, I, and M, 2nd U. S. Cav.; Cos. A, B, C, G, H, I, and K, 5th U. S. Infty.; Cos. C and K, 6th U. S. Infty.; Indian Scouts. Col. N. A. Miles in command. Soldiers killed, 3. Soldiers wounded, 3. Sitting Bull himself was present in this engagement.

July 19 .... Near Camp Loder, Mont. Detachment of Co. I, 7th U. S. Infty. Lieut. J. T. Van Orsdale in command. Indians killed, 1.

July 25 .... Near Salt Lake or Sulphur Springs, Texas. Detachment of Tr. H, 10th U. S. Cav.; Detachment of Co. H, 25 U. S. Infty. Capt. M. L. Courtney, 25th U. S. Infty., in command. Soldiers wounded, 2. Indians wounded, 3.

July 29 .... Vinegar Hill, Big Creek, Idaho. Co. C, and Detachment of Co. K, 2nd U. S. Infty. Lieut. Henry Catley in command. Soldiers wounded, 2.

July 27 .... Near Carrizo Mountains, Texas. Detachment of Tr. H, 10th U. S. Cav. Capt. M. L. Courtney in command. Soldiers wounded, 2. Indians wounded, 3. Ponies captured, 10.

August 4 .... Porcupine Creek, Mont. Detachment of Col. N. A. Miles command. Capt. Samuel Ovenshine in command. Arrested a band of half-breeds, capturing 143 carts and 193 horses. Next day 4 camps of half-breeds were arrested, numbering 308 carts.

August 10 .... Missouri River, near Popular Creek, Mont. Cos. A, B, C, G, H, I, and K, 5th U. S. Infty.; Tr. I, 2nd U. S. Cav. Lieut. Col. J. N. G. Whistler in command. Indians captured, 57. Ponies captured, 100. Surrender of Fast Bull.

August 19 .... Big Creek, Idaho. Indian Scouts.

August 20 .... Salmon River, Idaho. Detachment of Trs. D and G, 1st U. S. Cav. Capt. R. F. Bernard in command of force.

August 20 .... Soldier Bar or Big Creek, Idaho. Detachment of Trs. D and G, 1st U. S. Cav; Detachment of Co. C and Co. K, 2nd U. S. Infty. Sergeant of 2nd U. S. Infty and Corpl. Chas. B. Hardin, Co. G, 1st U. S. Cav., in command. Soldiers killed, 1, Private Harry Eagan of Co. C, 2nd U. S. Infty.

September 4 .... Ojo Caliente, N. M. Detachment of Tr. E, 9th U. S. Cav. Sergt. S. Chapman in command. Soldiers killed, 5. Citizens killed, 3.

September 10 .... McEver's Ranch, N. M. Citizens killed, 7.

September 10 .... Arroyo Seco, N. M. Citizens killed, 2.

September 16 .... Van Horn Mountains, Texas. Detachment of Tr. H, 10th U. S. Cav.; Co. H, 25th U. S. Infty. Capt. M. L. Courtney, 25th U. S. Infty., in command.

September 17 .... Black Range, N. M. Citizens killed, 2.

September 18 .... Las Animas River, N. M. Trs. A, B, C, G, 9th U. S. Cav. Capt. C. D. Beyer in command. Soldiers killed, 4. Citizens killed, 1. Soldiers wounded, 2.

September 19 .... Mimbres Mountains, N. M. Navajo Indian Scouts.

Lieut. R. T. Emmet, 9th U. S. Cav., in command. Soldiers killed, 2.

September 21 .... Big Meadow, Idaho. Indian Scouts.

September 22 .... Near Middle Fork, Salmon River, Idaho. Indian Scouts.

September 26-30 .... Near Ojo Caliente, Black Range, N. M. Detachments of the 6th and 9th U. S. Cav.; and Indian Scouts. Major A. P. Morrow, 9th U. S. Cav. in command. Soldiers killed, 1. Indians killed, 3.

September 29-October 1 .... Milk River, Colo. (White River Ute Expedition) Tr. E, 3rd U. S. Cav.; Trs. D and F, 5th U. S. Cav. Major T. T. Thornburgh, 4th U. S. Infty., and Capt. J. S. Payne, 5th U. S. Cav., in command. Major T. T. Thorburgh, 4th U. S. Infty., killed. Soldiers killed, 9. Citizens killed, 3. Capt. J. S. Payne and Lieut. J. V. S. Paddock, 5th U. S. Infty., and A. A. Surgeon R. B. Grimes, wounded. Soldiers wounded, 43. Citizens wounded, 3. Indians killed, 37.

September 29, 30 .... Cuchillo Negro River, Miembres Mountains, N. M. Major A. P. Morrow in command. Soldiers killed, 2.

September 30 .... Near Canada de Alamosa, N. M. Detachment of Tr. E, 9th U. S. Cav.

October 1-6 .... Chamberlain Basin, Idaho. Indian Scouts.

October 2-4 .... Milk Creek, Colo. Tr. E, 3rd U. S. Cav.; Trs. D and F, 5th U. S. Cav.; Tr. D, 9th U. S. Cav. Capt F. S. Dodge, 9th U. S. Cav., in command.

October 5 .... Milk Creek, Colo. Tr. E, 3rd U. S. Cav.; Trs. A, B, D, F, I, and M, 5th U. S. Cav.; Tr. D, 9th U. S. Cav.; Cos. B, C, E, F, and I, 4th U. S. Infty. Col. Wesley Merritt, 5th U. S. Cav., in command.

October 10 .... White River, Colo. Tr. E, 3rd U. S. Cav.; Trs. A, B, D, F, H, I, and M, 5th U. S. Cav.; Tr. D, 9th U. S. Cav.; Cos. B, C, E, F, and I, 4th U. S. Infty. Col Wesley Merritt, 5th U. S. Cav., in command.

October 13 .... Lloyd's Ranch, N. M. Soldiers killed, 6.

October 13 .... Slocum's Ranch, N. M. Citizens killed, 11.

October 20 .... Rifle Creek, near White River, Colo. Detachment of Tr. H, 5th U. S. Cav.; Indian Scouts. Lieut. W. P. Hall, 5th U. S. Cav., in command. Lieut. W. B. Weir, Ordnance Department, killed while hunting. Soldiers killed, 1. Indians killed, 2.

October 27 .... Guzman Mountains, near Corralitos River, Mexico. Detachment of Tr. A, 6th U. S. Cav.; Detachments of Trs. B, C, G, H, 9th U. S. Cav.; Indian Scouts. Major A. P. Morrow, 9th U. S. Cav., in command. Soldiers killed, 1. Soldiers wounded, 2.

1880

January 12 .... Rio Puerco, N. M. Trs. B, C, F, G, H, and M, 9th U. S. Cav. Major A. P. Morrow in command. Soldiers killed, 2. Soldiers wounded, 1. Fight was with Victoria and his band.

January 17 .... San Mateo Mountains, N. M. Trs. B, C, F, H, and M, 9th U. S. Cav. Major A. P. Morrow in command. Lieut. J.

H. French, 9th U. S. Cav., killed. Soldiers wounded, 2. Fight was with Victoria again.

January 30 .... Cabello Mountains, N. M. Detachments of Trs. B and M, 9th U. S. Cav. Capt. L. H. Rucker in command. Soldiers wounded, 3. Indians killed, 1.

February 3 .... San Andreas Mountains, N. M. Trs. B, C, F, H, and M, 9th U. S. Cav.; and Indian Scouts. Major A. P. Morrow, 9th U. S. Cav., in command. Soldiers wounded, 4.

February 6 .... Near Porcupine Creek, Mont. Crow Indian Scouts. Pursued and overtook a band of Sioux who had stolen horses from settlers in Pease's Bottom on the Yellowstone.

February 12 .... Near Pumpkin Creek, Mont. Detachment of Tr. B, 2nd U. S. Cav.; and Indian Scouts. Sergt. T. B. Glover in command. Soldiers killed, 1. Indians wounded, 2. Indians captured, 3.

February 28 .... Sacramento Mountains, N. M. Tr. A, 9th U. S. Cav. Lieut. John Conline in command.

March .... Near La Luz, N. M. Citizens killed, 3.

March 8 .... Porcupine Creek, Mont. Cos. I and K, 5th U. S. Infty. Capt. F. D. Baldwin in command.

March 8 .... Rosebud Creek, Mont. Detachment of Co. E, 5th U. S. Infty.; and Indian Scouts. Lieut. S. W. Miller in command. Soldiers killed, 2. Soldiers wounded, 1. Indians killed, 3. Killed 8 ponies. Destroyed the camp.

March 13 .... Near Russell's Ranch, Texas. Citizens killed, 1.

March 15 .... Blazer's Mill, N. M. Citizens killed, 1.

March 24 .... Near Ft. Custer, Mont. Tr. M, 2nd U. S. Cav. Capt. J. Mix in command. Recaptured 16 ponies.

April 1 .... O'Fallon's Creek, Mont. Detachments of Trs. C and E, 2nd U. S. Cav. Capt. E. L. Huggins in command. Soldiers killed, 1. Indians captured, 5. Captured 46 ponies, and some arms.

April 3 .... Near Pecos Falls, Texas. Trs. F and L, 10th U. S. Cav. Lieut. Calvin Esterly in command. Indians killed, 1. 8 head of stolen stock recovered.

April 5 .... San Andreas Mountains, N. M. (Miembrillo Canon) Tr. A, 9th U. S. Cav. Lieut. John Conline in command. Soldiers wounded, 1. Citizens wounded, 1.

April 6-9 .... San Andreas Mountains, N. M. (Miembrillo Canon) Trs. A, D, F, and G, 9th U. S. Cav. Capt. H. Carroll and Lieut. Patrick Cusack in command. Capt. H. Carroll wounded. Soldiers wounded, 7. Troops struck Victoria. Many of the Mescaleros and some Camanches were in the fight. Their trail was followed to the Mescalero Agency.

April 7 .... San Andreas Mountains, N. M. Detachments of Trs. D and E, 6th U. S. Cav., and Indian Scouts. Capt. C. B. McLellan in command.

April 9 .... Shakehand Springs, Texas. Tr. K, 10th U. S. Cav. Capt. T. C. Lebo in command. Indians killed, 1. Indians captured, 5. Killed the chief of the band, captured between 20 and 30 head of stock, destroyed the camp, and recovered a Mexican boy named Coyetano Gracia, who had been taken captive by the Indians.

April 15 .... Pato Spring, N. M. Citizens killed, 1.
April 16 .... Camp near South Fork, N. M. Detachment of Tr. G, 9th U. S. Cav.; Co. G, 15th U. S. Infty. Capt. Chas. Steelhammer, 15th U. S. Infty., in command. Indians killed, 1. Indians captured, 300.
April 16 .... Mescalero Agency, N. M. Detachments of Trs. H and L, 9th U. S. Cav.; Trs. D, E, F, K and L, 10th U. S. Cav.; and Detachments of 25th U. S. Infty. Col. Edward Hatch, 9th U. S. Cav., in command. Indians killed, 10. About 200 ponies and mules captured. About 200 Indians taken into the Agency.
April 17 .... Near Dog Canon, N. M. Tr. L, 6th U. S. Cav.; Tr. L, and D, 9th U. S. Cav.; Indian Scouts. Major A. P. Morrow, 9th U. S. Cav., in command. Indians killed, 3.
April 20 .... Sacramento Mountains, N. M. Detachment of Tr. L, 10th U. S. Cav. Lieut. M. M. Maxon in command. Indians killed, 1.
April 27 .... Near Ojo Caliente, N. M. Citizens killed, 3.
April 28 .... Near Head of Rio Gilitfe, N. M. Citizens killed, 6.
April 29 .... Mogollon Mountains, N. M. Citizens killed, 3.
May 2 .... San Francisco River, N. M. Citizens killed, 7.
May 4 .... Las Lentes, N. M. Citizens killed, 6.
May 7 .... Ash Creek Valley, Ariz. Detachment of Trs. E and D, 6th U. S. Cav.; Indian Scouts. Capt. Adam Kramer, 6th U. S. Cav., in command. Soldiers killed, 1. Soldiers wounded, 1.
May 13 .... Bass Canon, Texas. Citizens killed, 2. Citizens wounded, 2.
May 14 .... Old Ft. Tularosa, N. M. Detachments of Trs. E, I, and K, 9th U. S. Cav. Sergt. G. Jordan in command.
May 15 .... Kelly's Ranch, N. M. Citizens killed, 3.
May 24 .... Headwaters of Polomas River, N. M. Indian Scouts. Chief Scout H. K. Parker in command. Indians killed, 55.
May 29 .... Cook's Canon, N. M. Citizens killed, 5.
June 5 .... Cook's Canon, N. M. Trs. A, D, K, and L, 9th U. S. Cav. Major A. P. Morrow in command. Indians killed, 10. Indians wounded, 3. One of the killed was a son of Victoria.
June 11-12 .... Ojo Viejo, Texas. Detachment of Pueblo Scouts. Lieut. F. H. Milles, 24th U. S. Infty., in command. Soldiers killed, 1. Indians wounded, 2.
July 30 .... Rocky Ridge, or Eagles Pass, Texas. Detachments of Trs. A, C, D, and G, 10th U. S. Cav.; and Indian Scouts. Col. B. H. Grierson, 10th U. S. Cav., in command. Lieut. S. R. Collady wounded. Soldiers killed, 1. Soldiers wounded, 3. Indians killed, 7. Troops attacked by Victoria's Indians.
July 31 .... Near Eagle Springs, Texas. Stage driver and one passenger killed.
August 3 .... Sierra Diablo, Texas. Tr. K, 10th U. S. Cav. Capt. T. C. Lebo in command. Captured Victoria's supply camp of 25 head of cattle and other provisions.
August 3 .... Alamo Springs, Texas. Detachments of Trs. B, C, G, and H, 10th U. S. Cav.; and Indian Scouts. Corpl. Asa Weaver, Tr. H, 10th U. S. Cav., in command. Soldiers wounded, 1.

—89—

August 4 .... Camp Safford, Guadaloupe Mountains, Texas. De-
tachment of Tr. F, 10th U. S. Cav. Sergt. Wm. Richardson in
command. Soldiers killed, 1.
August 6 .... Guadaloupe Mountains, Texas. Tr. F, 10th U. S. Cav.
Capt. W. B. Kenedy in command. Indians killed, 2.
August 6 .... Near Rattlesnake Springs, Texas. Detachment of Tr. H,
10th U. S. Cav.; and Co. H, 24th U. S. Infty. Capt. J. C. Gil-
more, 24th U. S. Infty., in command. Indians Killed, 1.
Train guard attacked by the Indians but were repulsed.
August 6 .... Rattlesnake Canon, Texas. Detachment of Trs. B, C,
G, and H, 10th U. S. Cav. Capt. L. H. Carpenter, 10th U. S.
Cav., in command. Indians killed, 4.
August 9 .... Near old Ft. Quitman, Texas. Citizens killed, 1.
August 11 .... Near old Ft. Quitman, Texas. Tr. K, 8th U. S. Cav.;
Tr. A, 10th U. S. Cav.; some Lipan scouts and Texas rangers.
Capt. Nolan in command. Struck Victoria's band and pur-
sued them into Old Mexico.
August 17 .... Near the forks of the Box Elder Creek, Mont. De-
tachment of 8 men of Tr. F, 7th U. S. Cav.; and three Indian
Scouts. Sergt. Davern, Tr. F, 7th U. S. Cav., in command.
Indians killed, 2. Indians wounded, 1. Captured 7 head of
stock.
August 19 .... Mouth of O'Fallon's Creek, Mont. Indian Scouts. Re-
captured 11 head of stock.
September 1 .... Aqua Chiquita, Sacramento Mountains, N. M. Tr.
G, 9th U. S. Cav.; Detachment of Co. C, 15th U. S. Infty.
Sergt. J. Robinson, 9th U. S. Cav., in command. Soldiers
wounded, 2.
September 7 .... Near Ft. Cummings, N. M. Tr. A, 4th U. S. Cav.
Capt. L. O. Parker in command. Soldiers killed, 1. Soldiers
1. Soldiers wounded, 3.
September 8 .... Ft. Keogh, Mont. "Big Road" and 200 Sioux sur-
rendered to the commanding officer.
October 26 .... Ft. Stanton, N. M. 24 Apaches surrendered to the
commanding officer at the Mescalero Agency.
October 28 .... Ojo Caliente, Texas. Detachments of Trs. B, I, and
K, 10th U. S. Cav. Sergt. C. Perry in command. Soldiers
killed, 5. 35 to 40 Indians attacked a picket party.
November 11 .... Mouth of Musselshell River, Mont. Detachment of
Tr. M, 2nd U. S. Cav.; and Indian Scouts. Lieut. F. F. Kis-
lingbury, 11th U. S. Infty., in command. Indians killed, 1.
Attacked by a war party of Sioux.
December 2 .... Camp near South Fork in White Mountains, N. M.
Co. C, 15th U. S. Infty. Capt. C. H. Conrad in command.
Soldiers wounded, 2. Indians wounded, 1. Indians cap-
tured, 4.

1881

January 2 .... Poplar River, Mont. Surrender of hostiles. Tr. F,
7th U. S. Cav.; Cos. A, B, C, F, and G, 5th U. S. Infty.; Detachment of Co. A, 7th U. S. Infty.; and Co. F, 11th U. S.
Infty. Major Guido Ilges, 5th U. S. Infty., in command. In-

dians killed, 8. Indians captured, 324. Troops attacked camp of 400 Sioux. Captured 200 ponies, 69 guns and pistols.

January 24 .... Near Canada Alamosa, N. M. Detachment of Tr. D, 9th U. S. Cav. (Train guard.) Sergt. M. Ingoman in command. Soldiers wounded, 1.

January 29 .... Camp Poplar River, Mont. Major Guido Ilges, 5th U. S. Infty., in command. Indians captured, 64. Surrender of Iron Dog. Captured 8 lodges, 5 guns, 13 ponies.

February 5 .... Candelaria Mountains, Mexico. Detachment of Tr. K, 9th U. S. Cav.; Indian Scouts. Lieut. J. A. Maney, 15th U. S. Infty., in command.

February 12 .... Redwater, Yanktonnais Camp, Mont. Major Guido Ilges, 5th U. S. Infty., in command. Indians captured, 185. 15 horses and 7 guns were taken from the prisoners.

February 26 .... Ft. Buford, Dak. Surrender of hostile Sioux. Major D. H. Brotherton, 7th U. S. Infty., in command. Indians captured, 325. Captured 150 ponies and 40 guns and pistols.

April 11 .... Ft. Buford, Da. Surrender of hostiles. Major D. H. Brotherton, 7th U. S. Infty., in command. Indians captured, 135.

April 18 .... Ft. Keogh, Mont. Surrender of hostile Sioux. Lieut. Col. J. N. G. Whistler, 5th U. S. Infty., in command. Indians captured, 156. 32 lodges, 57 ponies, 16 guns and 3 revolvers taken by Lieut. Col. Whistler.

April 29 .... Near Mexican line, Ft. Cummings, N. M. Detachment of Tr. K, 9th U. S. Cav.; and Indian Scouts. Lieut. J. A. Maney, 15th U. S. Infty., in command. Soldiers killed, 1.

May 3 .... Sierra Burras Mountains, Mexico. Seminole Negro Scouts. Lieut. J. L. Bullis, 24th U. S. Infty., in command. Indians killed, 4. Indians captured, 2.

May 24 .... Camp Poplar River, Mont. Surrender of hostiles. Capt. O. B. Read, 11th U. S. Infty., in command. Indians captured, 50. 8 lodges of hostiles surrendered.

May 26 .... Ft. Buford, Dak. Surrender of hostiles. Major D. H. Brotherton, 7th U. S. Infty., in command. Indians captured, 32.

July 17 .... Alamo Canon, N. M. Detachment of Tr. L, 9th U. S. Cav.; Indian Scouts. Lieut. J. F. Guilfoyle in command. Citizens wounded, 1.

July 19 .... Arena Blanca, N. M. Detachment of Tr. L, 9th U. S. Cav.; Indian Scouts. Lieut. J. F. Guilfoyle in command. Citizens killed, 3.

July 20 .... Ft. Buford, Dak. Surrender of Sitting Bull and last of followers. Major D. H. Brotherton, 7th U. S. Infty., in command. Indians captured, 185.

July 25 .... San Andreas Mountains, N. M. Detachment of Tr. L, 9th U. S. Cav.; Indian Scouts. Lieut. J. F. Guilfoyle in command. Citizens wounded, 3. Indians killed, 2.

July 25 .... White Sands, N. M. Detachment of Tr. L, 9th U. S. Cav.; Indian Scouts.

July 26 .... San Andreas Mountains, N. M. Detachment of Tr. L,

9th U. S. Cav.; Indian Scouts. Lieut. J. F. Guilfoyle in command.

July 30 .... San Mateo Mountains, N. M. Citizens killed, 4.

August 1 .... Red Canon of San Mateo Mountains, N. M. Citizens killed, 1. Citizens wounded, 7.

August 3 .... Monica Springs, N. M. Detachment of Tr. L, 9th U. S. Cav.; Indian Scouts. Lieut. J. F. Guilfoyle in command. Indians wounded, 2.

August 12 .... Carrizo Canon, N. M. Detachment of Tr. K, 9th U. S. Cav. Capt. Chas. Parker in command. Soldiers wounded, 2. Soldiers wounded, 3. Indians killed, 4.

August 15 .... Rio Cuchilly Negro, N. M. Tr. I, 9th U. S. Cav. Lieut. Gustavus Valois in command. Lieut. G. R. Burnett wounded. Soldiers wounded, 2.

August 16 .... Near San Mateo Mountains, Black Range, N. M. Detachments of Trs. B, and H, 9th U. S. Cav.; Indian Scouts. Lieut. C. W. Taylor, 9th U. S. Cav., in command.

August 19 .... McEvers' Ranch in Guerillo Canon, N. M. Detachments of Trs. B and F, 9th U. S. Cav.; and citizen volunteers. Lieut. G. W. Smith in command. 2nd Lieut. G. W. Smith, 9th U. S. Cav., killed. Soldiers killed, 3. Citizens killed, 1. Soldiers wounded, 3.

August 30 .... Cibicu Creek, Ariz. Tr. D and E, 6th U. S. Cav.; Indian Scouts. Col. E. A. Carr, 6th U. S. Cav., in command. Capt. E. C. Hentig, 6th U. S. Cav., killed. Soldiers killed, 5. Soldiers wounded, 3. Citizens wounded, 1.

August 31 .... Near Ft. Apache, Ariz. Detachment of Tr. D, 6th U. S. Cav.; Detachment of Co. D, 12th U. S. Infty. Soldiers killed, 3. Citizens killed, 5.

September 1 .... Ft. Apache, Ariz. Trs. D and E, 6th U. S. Cav.; Co. D, 12th U. S. Infty.; Indian Scouts. Col. E. A. Carr, 6th U. S. Cav., in command. Lieut. C. G. Gordon, 6th U. S. Cav., wounded.

September 30 .... San Carlos, Ariz. Trs. A, B, C, and E, 6th U. S. Cav. Col. E. A. Carr, 6th U. S. Cav., in command. Indians captured, 47.

October 2 .... Cedar Springs, Ariz. Tr. G, 1st U. S. Cav.; Trs. A and F, 6th U. S. Cav.; Indian Scouts. Col. O. B. Willcox, 12th U. S. Infty., in command. Soldiers killed, 3. Soldiers wounded, 3.

October 4 .... South Pass of Dragoon Mountains, Ariz. Trs. G and I, 1st U. S. Cav.; Trs. F, H, and D, 9th U. S. Cav.; Indian Scouts. Col. O. B. Willcox, 12th U. S. Infty., in command. Fight with Chiricahue Apache Indians.

October 8 .... Near Milk River, Mont. Trs. H, and L, 2nd U. S. Cav. Capt. Randolph Norwood in command.

November 3 .... Canyon Creek, Ariz. Indian Scouts.

1882

April 20 .... Near Milk River, Mont. Trs. H and L, 2nd U. S. Cav.

April 20 .... Near Ft. Thomas, Ariz. Tr. B, 6th U. S. Cav. Lieut. G. H. Sands in command. Indians wounded, 1.

April 23 .... Near Stein's Pass, Ariz. Detachment of Tr. M, 4th U.

S. Cav.; Indian Scouts. Lieut. D. N. McDonald, 4th U. S. Cav., in command. Soldiers killed, 4.

April 23 ...... Horseshoe Canon, N. M. Trs. C, F, G, H, and M, 4th U. S. Cav.; Indian Scouts. Lieut. Col. G. A. Forsyth, 4th U. S. Cav., in command. Lieut. J. W. Martin, 4th U. S. Cav., wounded. Soldiers killed, 1. Soldiers wounded, 6. Indians killed, 13.

April 28 ...... Hatchet Mountains, near Mexican Line, N. M. Trs. G and M, 6th U. S. Cav.; and Cos. B and D, Indian Scouts. Capt. T. C. Tupper, 6th U. S. Cav., in command. Soldiers killed, 1. Soldiers wounded, 2. Indians killed, 6. Captured 72 head of stock.

April 29 ...... Shoshone Agency, near Ft. Washakie, Wyo. Detachments of Tr. H and K, 3rd U. S. Cav.; and Indian Scouts. Lieut. G. H. Morgan, 3rd U. S. Cav., in command. Soldiers killed, 1. Indians killed, 1. Death of Ute chief, Captain Jack.

June 1 ...... In canon near Cloverdale, N. M. Trs. A, and C, 6th U. S. Cav.; Indian Scouts. Lieut. Wm. Stanton, 6th U. S. Cav., in command. Indians killed, 2.

July 9 ...... Medicine Lodge, Mont. Tr. L, 2nd U. S. Cav. Capt. Randolph Norwood in command.

July 23 ...... Agency at Ft. Stanton, N. M. Indian police. Citizens wounded, 1. Indians killed, 3.

August 15 ...... Near Ft. Apache, Ariz. Indian Scouts.

November 8 ...... Near Tullock's Fork, Mont. Indian Scouts. Soldiers wounded, 1. Indians killed, 2.

1883

March 21 ...... 12 miles South West of Ft. Huachuca, Ariz. Citizens killed, 4.

March 22 ...... West side of Whetstone Mountains, Total Wreck Mine, Ariz. Citizens killed, 3.

March 23 ...... Point of Mountain, south end Galiuro Range, Ariz. Citizens killed, 2.

March 28 ...... Between Silver City and Lordsburg, N. M. Citizens killed, 2.

April 14 ...... Beaver Creek, or Sweetgrass Hills, Mont. Detachment of Tr. H, 2nd U. S. Cav. Capt. M. E. O'Brien in command. Indians captured, 69.

April 19 ...... Wild Horse Lake, near boundary of British territory, Mont. Detachment of Tr. L, 2nd U. S. Cav. Capt. Randolph Norwood in command. Indians killed, 2.

May 15 ...... Babispe River, in Sierra Madre, Mexico. Cos. A, B, C, D, E, F, and G, Indian Scouts. Capt. Emmet Crawford, 3rd U. S. Cav., in command. Crook's Expedition. Indians killed, 9. Indians captured, 5.

1884

July 15 ...... Wormington Canyon, Colo. Trs. B and F, 6th U. S. Cav. Lieut. H. P. Perrine in command. Citizens killed, 2.

May 22 .... Devil's Creek, Mogollon Mountains, N. M. Trs. A and K, 4th U. S. Cav.; Indian Scouts. Capt. Allen Smith, 4th U. S. Cav., in command. Soldiers wounded, 4.

June 8 .... Guadalupe Canyon, Sonora, Mexico. Detachments of Trs. C, D, and G, 4th U. S. Cav. Supply train guard. Soldiers killed, 3.

June 21 .... Oputo, Sonora, Mexico. Detachment of Co. D, Indian Scouts. Lieut. Britton Davis, 3rd U. S. Cav., in command. Soldiers killed, 1.

June 23 .... Babispe Mountains, Sonora, Mexico. Detachments of 3rd and 6th U. S. Cav.; Indian Scouts. Capt. Emmet Crawford, 3rd U. S. Cav., in command. Indians killed, 1. Indians captured, 15.

July 28 .... Sierra Madre, Sonora, Mexico. Detachments of Cos. G, H, and K, Indian Scouts. Capt. Wirt Davis, 4th U. S. Cav., in command. Indians killed, 2.

August 7 .... Sierra Madre, Sonora, Mexico. Detachment of Cos. G, H, I, and K, Indian Scouts. Capt. Wirt Davis, 4th U. S. Cav., in command. Indians killed, 5. Indians captured, 15.

September 22 .... Teres Mountains, Mexico. Detachments of Cos. G, H, I, and K, Indian Scouts. Capt. Wirt Davis, 4th U. S. Cav., in command. Soldiers killed, 1. Soldiers wounded, 1. Indians killed, 1. Indians wounded, 2.

October 10 .... Near Lang's ranch, N. M. Detachment of Tr. F, 4th U. S. Cav. (courier). Soldiers killed, 1.

November 8 .... Florida Mountains, N. M. Tr. A, 6th U. S. Cav.; Indian Scouts. Soldiers killed, 1. Soldiers wounded, 1.

December 9 .... Lillie's Ranch, on Clear Creek, N. M. Tr. C, 8th U. S. Cav. Lieut. S. W. Fountain in command. Indians killed, 2.

December 19 .... Little Dry Creek, or White House, N. M. Tr. C, 8th U. S. Cav. Lieut. S. W. Fountain in command. Asst. Surg. T. J. C. Maddox killed. Soldiers killed, 4. Lieut. De R. C. Cabell, 8th U. S. Cav., wounded. Soldiers wounded, 1.

1886

January 10—11 .... Near Aros River, Sonora, Mexico. Cos. A, B, and C, Indian Scouts. Capt. Emmet Crawford, 3rd U. S. Cav., in command. Capt. E. Crawford, 3rd U. S. Cav., wounded by Mexican troops, died January 18, 1886.

May 3 .... Near Penito Mountains, Sonora, Mexico. Tr. K, 10th U. S. Cav. Capt. T. C. Lebo in command. Soldiers killed, 1. Soldiers wounded, 1. Indians killed, 2. Indians captured, 1.

May 15 .... Pinto Mountains, or Santa Cruz Mountains, Mexico. Tr. D, 4th U. S. Cav. Capt. C. A. P. Hatfield in command. Soldiers killed, 2. Soldiers wounded, 2.

June 6 .... Patagonia Mountains, Ariz. Tr. B, 4th U. S. Cav. Lieut. R. D. Walsh in command.

July 13 .... Yakin River, Mexico. Detachments of Cos. D and K, 8th U. S. Infty.; and Indian Scouts. Capt. H. W. Lawton, 4th U. S. Cav., in command.

September 4 .... Skeleton Canon, Ariz. Brig. Gen. N. A. Miles in command. Indians captured, 39. Surrender of Geronimo.
October 18 .... Black River Mountains, Ariz. Tr. H, 10th U. S. Cav. Capt. C. L. Cooper in command. Indians captured, 8.

1887

March 10 .... San Carlos Agency, Ariz. Lieut. Seward Mott, 10th U. S. Cav., died from wound, March 11, 1887.
June 11 .... Rincon Mountains, Ariz. Detachments of Trs. E and L, 10th U. S. Cav. Lieut. C. P. Johnson in command.
November 5 .... Crow Agency, Mont. Trs. A, B, D, E, G, and K, 1st U. S. Cav.; Tr. A, 7th U. S. Cav.; Tr. H, 9th U. S. Cav.; Co. B, and E, 3rd U. S. Infty.; Cos. D, G, and I, 5th U. S. Infty.; Co. C, 7th U. S. Infty. Brig. Gen. T. H. Ruger in command. Soldiers killed, 1. Soldiers wounded, 2. Indians killed, 7. Indians wounded, 10. Indians captured, 9.

1888

June 16 .... Pompey's Pillar on Yellowstone River, Mont. Detachment of Indian Scouts. Interpreter C. Cacely in command. Indians killed, 1. Indians wounded, 1.
July 28 .... Near San Carlos Agency, Ariz. Indian Scouts—herding. Soldiers wounded, 2.

1889

May 11 .... Cedar Springs, Ariz. Detachments of Trs. C and G, 10th U. S. Cav.; Detachments of Cos. B, C, E, and K, 24th U. S. Infty. Escort duty. Sergt. B. Brown, 24th U. S. Infty., commanding escort for Paymaster J. W. Wham. Soldiers wounded, 9.
June 2 .... North bank of Missouri River, 15 miles from mouth of Little Missouri River, N. D. Tr. K, 8th U. S. Cav. Capt. H. W. Sprole in command. Indians captured, 34.

1890

March 11 .... Salt River, near mouth of Cherry Creek, Ariz. Detachment of Tr. L, 4th U. S. Cav.; Detachment of Tr. K, 10th U. S. Cav.; and Indian Scouts. Lieut. J. W. Watson, 10th U. S. Cav., in command. Indians killed, 2. Indians captured, 3.
September 13 .... Tongue River Agency, Mont. Trs. E and G, 1st U. S. Cav. Lieut. John Pitcher in command. Indians killed, 2.
December 15 .... Grand River, near Standing Rock, Mont. Trs. F and G, 8th U. S. Cav.; and Indian Police. Capt. E. G. Fechet, 8th U. S. Cav., in command. Soldiers killed, 4. Soldiers wounded, 3. Indians killed, 8.
December 21—22 .... Retamal, Texas. Detachment of Tr. C, 3rd U. S. Cav.; and Co. E, 18th U. S. Infty.
December 22 .... Cherry Creek, S. D. Capt. J. H. Hurst, 12th U. S. Infty., in command. Indians captured, 294. Surrender of "Sitting Bull's" band.
December 28 .... Near Porcupine Creek, S. D. Trs. A, B, I, and K, 7th U. S. Cav.; Detachment of Bat. E, 1st U. S. Artillery. Major S. M. Whitside, 7th U. S. Cav., in command. Indians captured, 106. Capture of "Big Foot's" band.

December 29 .... Pine Ridge Agency, S. D. 2nd U. S. Infty. Col.
Frank Wheaton in command. Soldiers wounded, 3.

December 29 .... Wounded Knee Creek, S. D. Trs. A, B, C, D, E, G,
I, and K, 7th U. S. Cav.; Bat. E, 1st U. S. Artillery; Indian
Scouts. Col. J. W. Forsyth, 7th U. S. Cav., in command.
Capt. G. D. Wallace, 7th U. S. Cav., killed. Soldiers killed,
24. Lieuts. E. A. Garlington, J. C. Gresham, 7th U. S. Cav.,
and Lieut. H. L. Hawthorne, 2nd Artillery, wounded. Soldiers wounded, 32. Indians killed, 128. Indians wounded,
33.

December 30 .... Near Pine Ridge Agency, S. D. Tr. D, 9th U. S.
Cav. Capt. J. S. Loud in command. Soldiers killed, 1. Attack on wagon train.

December 30 .... Near Pine Ridge Agency, S. D. Trs. E, I, and K,
9th U. S. Cav.

December 30 .... White Clay Creek or old Catholic Mission, S. D.
Trs. A, B, C, D, E, G, I, and K, 7th U. S. Cav.; Trs. D, E, I,
and K, 9th U. S. Cav.; Bat. E, 1st U. S. Artillery; Indian
Scouts. Col. J. W. Forsyth, 7th U. S. Cav., in command.
Soldiers killed, 1. Lieut. J. D. Mann, 7th U. S. Cav., wound-
ed. Soldiers wounded, 6.

1891

January 1 .... Near Wounded Knee Creek, S. D. Tr. K, 6th U. S.
Cav. Capt. J. B. Kerr in command. Indians killed, 4. Indians
wounded, 4.

January 1 .... Near mouth of Little Grass Creek, S. D. Trs. A, F, H,
I and K, 6th U. S. Cav.

January 7 .... Near Pine Ridge Agency, S. D. Detachment of Indian
Scouts. Lieut. E. W. Casey, 22nd U. S. Infty., in command.
Lieut. E. W. Casey killed by Brule Indians.

January 9 .... Near Ft. Buford, N. D. Detachment of Tr. E, 8th U.
S. Cav.

December 21—22 .... Retamal, Texas. Detachment of Tr. C, 3rd U.
S. Cav.; and Co. E, 18th U. S. Infty.

December 29 .... Charco Renondo, Texas. Detachment of Tr. C, 3rd
U. S. Cav.

December 30 .... Rancho Rendado Zapata, Texas. Trs. A and G,
3rd U. S. Cav.

1892

January 24 .... Rancho Grominito, Texas. Detachment of Tr. C, 3rd
U. S. Cav.

February 6—15 .... Near Grande, Texas. Detachment of Tr. C, 3rd
U. S. Cav.

February 18 .... Northeast of Palito Blanco, Texas. Tr. D, 3rd U. S.
Cav.

December 24 .... El Alazan, near Roma, Texas. Tr. I, 3rd U. S. Cav.;
Indian Scouts.

1893

January 21 .... Near Baluarte Ranche, Texas. (Julian Guerras Pas-
tunte) Detachments of Trs. D, and K, 3rd U. S. Cav.

January 22 .... Las Tajitos ranch, near Brownsville, Texas. Detachments of Trs. D, and K, 3rd U. S. Cav.

February 23 .... Las Mulas ranch, Starr County, Texas. 30 miles north of Ft. Ringgold. Seminole scouts.

1896

May 8 .... Guadalupe Canyon, Ariz. Detachment of Tr. E, 7th U. S. Cav.; Indian Scouts.

June 21 .... Guadalupe Canyon, Ariz. Detachment of Tr. A, 1st U. S. Cav. Skirmish with band of Apaches.

1897

May 16 .... In mountains near Lang's ranch, Ariz. Detachments of Trs. C, E, and I, 7th U. S. Cav.; Indian Scouts.

INDEX

—135—

FORTS